"The recent pandemic took an unprecedented and catastrophic toll on the health, economy and mental wellbeing of the people globally. This has forced academics to revisit the disjunctive form of multidisciplinary research and theories. Professor Choudhury's elaborate discussion on the model of inclusiveness provides a fresh alternative and his collaborative work emanates from a place of faith, yet is explained with well-described theories. His model of social justice denotes a holistic approach towards a rights-based financial sustainability wherein protection towards the vulnerable and the marginalized people is ensured through effective participation."

– **Md. Monzur Rabbi**, *LL.M., International Arbitration, White & Case International Arbitration LL.M., University of Miami School of Law, Florida, USA; Barrister-at-Law (Lincoln's Inn, UK); Advocate, Supreme Court of Bangladesh. Mr. Rabbi is a member of the Honorable Society of Lincoln's Inn and was called to the Bar of England and Wales. He did his postgraduate degree on international arbitration from the University of Miami with a Fulbright Scholarship.*

Islamic Economics and COVID-19

This book is a timely exploration of an unprecedented, cataclysmic pandemic episode. It examines certain critical aspects of socio-scientific theory across a variety of diverse themes and through an epistemic lens.

The book investigates the general theory of pandemic episodes and their adverse long-term effects on human and environmental wellbeing. It includes an in-depth study of COVID-19 but also looks to the future to contemplate potential pandemics to come.

The existing approach to the study of pandemics is critically examined in terms of the prevalent isolated and thus mutated way of viewing human and mechanical relations in the name of specialization and modernity. The book presents a novel model of science-economy-society moral inclusiveness that forms a distinctive theoretical approach to the issue of normalizing all forms of pandemic challenges. It is methodologically different from existing economic theory, including the critical study of microeconomic foundations of macroeconomics. Human and environmental existence along with its multidisciplinary outlook of unity of knowledge between modernity, traditionalism, and socio-cultural values is emphasized in the treatment and cure of pandemic episodes.

The book is a unique reference work, offering fresh wisdom within the moral methodological worldview.

Masudul Alam Choudhury is International Chair in Islamic Economics and Finance in the Faculty of Economics, Trisakti University, Jakarta, Indonesia.

Routledge Focus on Economics and Finance

The fields of economics are constantly expanding and evolving. This growth presents challenges for readers trying to keep up with the latest important insights. Routledge Focus on Economics and Finance presents short books on the latest big topics, linking in with the most cutting-edge economics research.

Individually, each title in the series provides coverage of a key academic topic, whilst collectively the series forms a comprehensive collection across the whole spectrum of economics.

For more information about this series, please visit www.routledge.com/ Routledge-Focus-on-Economics-and-Finance/book-series/RFEF

Islamic Economics and COVID-19

The Economic, Social and Scientific Consequences of a Global Pandemic

Masudul Alam Choudhury

With the cooperation of
Participants of the Three Online
Forums on Global Pandemic Episode 2020

SELECTED LIST OF PARTICIPANTS IN THE ONLINE GLOBAL FORUMS (3) ON COVID-19 PANDEMIC EPISODES

Professor Masudul Alam Choudhury, Global Forums Organizer; International Chair, Postgraduate Program in Islamic Economics & Finance (IEF), Faculty of Economics, Trisakti University, Jakarta, Indonesia

Rodney Shakespeare, former Visiting Professor of Binary Economics, IEF, Trisakti University

Professor M. Shamsher Ali, Theoretical Nuclear Physicist, Emeritus Professor, Southeast University and Founder Vice-Chancellor, Bangladesh Open University

Professor Ishaq Bhatti, Director of Islamic Banking and Finance Program; Graduate Research Coordinator, Department of Economics, Finance and Marketing, La Trobe University, Melbourne, Australia

Professor Toseef Azid, College of Business and Economics, Qassim University, Saudi Arabia

Mr. Mahfuzul Alam Taifur, Department of Shari'ah and Economics, Institute of Islamic Studies, University of Malaya

Professor Jadi Suriadi, Researcher, The Wellbeing Institute, Jakarta, Indonesia

Professor Abdulkader Cassim Mahomedy, Lecturer, School of Accounting, Economics and Finance, University of KwaZulu-Natal, Durham, Republic of South Africa

Professor Abdul Ghafar Ismail, Professor of Financial Islamic Economics, Faculty of Economics and Muamalat, Universiti Sains Islam Malaysia, Malaysia

Professor Lubna Sarwath, State General Secretary and Spokesperson, Socialist Party (India), Hyderabad, India; Editorial Assistant, International Journal of Ethics and Systems, Emerald Publications, UK

Professor Ari Pratiwi, Post Graduate Lecturer in Management Department, Universitas Paramadina, Jakarta, Indonesia

Professor Nirdukita Ratnawati, Lecturer in Islamic Economic and Finance, Faculty of Economics & Business, Trisakti University, Jakarta, Indonesia

Professor Nur Hilmiyah, Department of Economics and Business, University of Pancasila, Jakarta, Indonesia

Professor Akhmad Affandi Mahfudz, CPIF, Lecturer of Islamic Economics Law, Postgraduate Studies University of Darussalam Gontor, Indonesia IEF postgraduate students 2020

Routledge
Taylor & Francis Group

LONDON AND NEW YORK

First published 2021
by Routledge
2 Park Square, Milton Park, Abingdon, Oxon OX14 4RN

and by Routledge
52 Vanderbilt Avenue, New York, NY 10017

Routledge is an imprint of the Taylor & Francis Group, an informa business

British Library Cataloguing-in-Publication Data
A catalogue record for this book is available from the British Library

Library of Congress Cataloging-in-Publication Data
Names: Choudhury, Masudul Alam, 1948– author.
Title: Islamic economics and COVID-19 : the economic, social and scientific consequences of a global pandemic / Masudul Alam Choudhury ; with the cooperation of participants of the three online forums on global pandemic episode 2020.
Description: Abingdon, Oxon ; New York, NY : Routledge, 2021. | Series: Routledge focus on economics and finance | Includes bibliographical references and index.
Identifiers: LCCN 2020048043 (print) | LCCN 2020048044 (ebook)
Subjects: LCSH: COVID-19 (Disease)—Economic aspects. | COVID-19 (Disease)—Social aspects. | COVID-19 (Disease)—Epidemiology—Methodology. | Economics—Religious aspects—Islam—Qur'anic teaching. | Economics—Statistical methods. | Economics—Methodology. | Epidemiology—Mathematical models.
Classification: LCC RA644.C67 C48 2021 (print) | LCC RA644.C67 (ebook) | DDC 362.1962/414—dc23
LC record available at https://lccn.loc.gov/2020048043
LC ebook record available at https://lccn.loc.gov/2020048044

ISBN: 978-0-367-74914-9 (hbk)
ISBN: 978-1-003-16022-9 (ebk)

Typeset in Times New Roman
by Apex CoVantage, LLC

Prelude

(Qur'an, 94, 5&6, Sharh, The Expansion)
So, surely with hardship comes ease.
Surely with difficulty comes ease.

Contents

Tables

Figures

Acknowledgement

My sincere thanks are to Routledge that reviewed this manuscript and promptly offered me the publishing contract on this book. My thanks are also to the various participants, those named in this manuscript and others, who attended the online Global Forum on COVID-19, three of them. Their scholarly verbal participation certainly helped me to include them in this manuscript. The manuscript though is my own complete work. Many thanks are to respected Barrister-at-Law Mr. Md. Monzur Rabbi, for his precise blurb on the content of this manuscript.

Masudul Alam Choudhury

Preface

By the will of divine providence, the novel pandemic of COVID-19 has come upon humankind with unprecedented ravages of disease, health problems, death, pestilence, and socio-economic disruptions. These maladies together make COVID-19's pandemic consequences to be the worst one after the Spanish Flu of 1918–1920, and the worst economically hit after the Great Depression of 1929–1932.

On the economic front, the worsening condition during COVID-19 is continuing with alarming spectre. During the Great Depression, gross domestic product (GDP) declined from $105 billion in 1929 to $57 billion in 1932. Economic devaluation remained at 30%. Thereby, Western economies were forced to borrow to pay their debts and for recovery of investments to mobilize the accumulated bank savings that remained underutilized even as investment remained lower than savings during the Great Depression. On the side of joblessness, unemployment rate stood at 24.9% by 1932.

During the present COVID-19 times, the US unemployment is predicted to stand at 32% by the end of 2020. US GDP declined by 4.8% during the first quarter of 2020. These grim statistics for the US society and economy bring to a close the longest epoch of American prosperity and economic security. The future prospects are equally dismal in prediction. European Union GDP is forecasted to decline by 7.5% by the end of 2020. Chinese economy is forecasted to shrink by 6%. The International Monetary Fund (IMF) forecasts a 0% rate of growth for Asian economies. This is a record stagnation for the first time in 60 years.

Thus, the pandemic is to be construed not simply as a medical catastrophe. A great destabilizing pandemic also shakes up the core of ensuing problems. Examples of pandemic consequences are felt on the economic and social fronts with long-term disabling. Examples are economic destruction and intensifying poverty, deprivation, inequality, and misery among the globally deprived, especially in developing countries. In this work we have encompassed the pandemic effects by its general theory and included in it the vastest pandemic effects. The outlook of pandemic treatment and cure is thereby taken beyond simply the science and medical fronts in terms of their modernization concepts.[1]

Such an integrated alternative medicinal treatment and cure has its distinctive place in our proposed model of science-economy-society moral inclusiveness in this study.

In this work the conjoint terminology 'science-economy-society moral inclusiveness' is used to mean interactive, integrative, and evolutionary learning interrelations between these multidisciplinary systems of intellection by way of their unified explanatory multivariates. Such a methodological inter-systemic unification between the multidisciplines is accomplished by the episteme of unity of knowledge. In our special case by the principle of universality and uniqueness for the treatment and control of pandemic the epistemic methodology is derived from the Qur'an in terms of the law of Tawhid, meaning monotheistic law of oneness.[2] This is represented in respect of the unity of knowledge in the generality and particulars of the world-system as the all-comprehensive moral domains joined together. In our case this world-system comprises the domain of pandemic study and its various long-term and deepening consequences that destroy global wellbeing. It was indeed the request from the post-doctoral graduates of the Postgraduate Program in Islamic Economics and Finance, Trisakti University, Jakarta, Indonesia, at the organized Global Forum to bring out the theory and application of Tawhid as the ontological law of monotheistic oneness in regard to COVID-19 in particular and the general case of pandemic episode along with its multifarious adversities. This book has resulted therefrom.

In the regime of COVID-19 pandemic there is still a gleaming of silver lining bordering the dark clouds of reality. It is that new epistemological worldview has taken shape in soul, mind, and matter to discern, explain, and combat global problems of catastrophic proportions. Such emergent epistemic methodological worldview is the new uniquely universal foundational origin of multidisciplinary details of 'everything.' A pandemic episode has a multidimensional nature. Within this scheme and shape of things as they presently are and will be in the future of pandemic realities science, economics, and society will know the origin of pandemic species in terms of the epistemic core of new thought. This ontological origin must then be formalized, applied, and sustained in terms of the knowledge of the inherently unique and universal worldview.

This aspect of the work establishes the substantive conclusion that the epistemic worldview towards formulating the emergent new approach to pandemic studies proves the validity of yet one more analytical formalism of the ontology of unity of knowledge between the good things of life to combat and reject the unwanted ones. Such an ontological worldview is claimed to arise from the Islamic premise of the Qur'an. It forms the epistemic study of Tawhid (monotheism) as law in the order and scheme of 'everything.' This is specified for COVID-19 as pandemic and generalized for all pandemic episodes and their severe maladies that all together inhibit wellbeing.

Thus, in the methodological approach of comprehensive treatment and cure of pandemic episodes and their adverse consequences the multidisciplinary perspective of integrating diverse fields of pandemic treatment and cure is accomplished by advancing the epistemic theory and application of specifics as they are governed by the episteme of unity of knowledge. This methodology is critically concluded to be the only way to attain the wellbeing objective by science-economy-society model of moral inclusiveness for pandemic treatment and control both now (COVID-19) and in the future. Along with these physical pandemic episodes there are various pandemic-like consequences, such as the monstrous existence of global poverty, extensive financial losses by non-performing loans and human deprivation, inequality, disempowerment, disenfranchisement, unemployment, protracted economic, social malaise, and the like.[3]

The permanent epistemic meaning of the multidisciplinary perspective of unity of knowledge and its contrariety in 'everything' will emerge for the wellbeing of intellection and its conscious application for the common good. The two contrary ways to view pandemic reality will be first, the way it is presently viewed in science, economy, and society in the absence of moral inclusiveness; and second, with moral inclusiveness embedded in the new epistemic scope of knowledge of the unified multidisciplinary field. The epistemic methodological worldview of multidisciplinary ensemble of unity of knowledge will offer the unique and universal knowledge of causality of being and becoming to wellbeing and reformation of normalcy away from abnormality (mutation) in pandemic 'everything.'

Figure 0.1 depicts such a dynamic convergence from mutation of pandemic episodes to normalcy of healthy life. 'E' denotes the regime of pandemic episodes and their degrading consequences. 'M' denotes the phenomenon of pandemic physical mutation. 'θ' denotes measured degree of wellbeing as normalcy occurs. The origin 'O' denotes negation of life in its state of perfect loss of immunity. At the point 'O' either 'M' or 'N' is at their maximum while the other attribute remains at its minimum. Life is possible in the configured (M,N)-pandemic region of present and future. The paths of convergence M $\rightarrow$ N are evolutionary learnt paths across regions of intra-systemic and inter-systemic interaction, leading to integration shown by n-dimensional circles. Indeed, the whole Figure 0.1 is situated in the n-dimensions of knowledge, space, and time.

The meaning of mutation also conveys human and systemic methodological individualism and multidisciplinary isolationism. The transformation

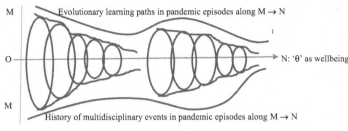

Figure 0.1 The learning world-system from mutation to normalcy and onwards of pandemic states in terms of Tawhidi configuration

between 'M' and 'N' by degrees occurs by the continuous repetition of learning in response to the episteme of unity of knowledge. The epistemic universality and uniqueness of ontological origin and continuity (sustainability) of being and becoming of explainable 'everything' is referred to in the Qur'an as the Tawhidi law of monotheistic oneness. Tawhid as law presents and explains itself in the details of the world-system by organic pairing of relations between all interacting, integrating, and thereby evolutionary learning entities of diversely multidisciplinary systems. In such shape and form they manifest the blessed choices while rejecting the vile ones opposing wellbeing (complementarities).

Thus, the previously noted adversities of COVID-19, future pandemic episodes to come, and their harsh consequences depriving global wellbeing will present a new epistemic methodological worldview to revert from pandemic properties of mutation and all systemic human individualism into renormalization of wellbeing. This will be possible with regard to the episteme of unity of knowledge between science, economy, and society and their varied consequences. The new epistemic methodological worldview will point out that a control of any form of future pandemic – with mutations of coronavirus or otherwise – will require healing by complementing all the good sides. This indeed conveys the substantive meaning of moral inclusiveness in the socio-scientific multidisciplinary ensemble of 'everything.'

This quest for profound change to arrest the existing pandemic regime and to control future pandemic episodes is not presently found in the existing dissociative model of science, society, economic, and business ideas. Science-economy-society unified relations of moral inclusiveness must persist in the epistemic worldview as it has continued on in the human comprehension of wellbeing and human ecological balance. Contrarily, the modernist socio-scientific thought prevails in properties of self-centeredness and methodological individualism. What has continued on in persistence of the old worldview of pandemic control based on materiality, scientific exclusiveness, and intensifying of behaviour of methodological individualism in economic and business psychology has culminated over time into a dissipated multidisciplinary episteme of isolationist thinking.

Thereby, the ethos of epistemic thought and its practice based on marginalism and individualism have continued in the isolated understanding of multidisciplinarity in science-economy-society relationship by the absence of moral inclusiveness. The emergent objectives of socio-scientific worldview are being pursued that are of the individuated nature. Pursuit of goals of maximization of wealth, ownership, and sanctified esoteric belief on self-centeredness has continued without respect of the coexisting values of communitarianism including all the other partners, be these animate or inanimate entities. To banish this gap of materiality and self-centeredness with only a notion and outwardly call for ethical behaviour by its enforcement of extraneous policies, institutions, and instrumental compulsion have existed. Such social conduct conveys the meaning of ethical exogeneity or exogenous ethics. Such a psychology and behaviour are contrary to the conscious moral episteme and practice of values as they are driven by the episteme of moral consciousness. This latter precept of learning with the moral consciousness of coexistence in the form of inter-agency organic participatory interrelations is required for a socio-scientific understanding of a new episteme. This is the principle of consilience, meaning unity of knowledge. Upon this methodological worldview the holism of moral inclusiveness must be conceptualized and applied to the entire socio-scientific domain with its specifics. The important grand domain is of science-economy-society with moral inclusiveness.

In this work we have explored the essential yet new revisiting of the ontology of unity of knowledge. This work also points out the missing gap in the modelling of pandemic treatment, cure, and control by the existing approach of dissociative multidisciplines. The ensuing structure of discussion, formalism, and applicative scenario of this approach to modelling pandemic cause, treatment, and control in their generalized comprehension of origins and consequences is studied in this work in an analytical fold. The entire epistemic outlook of such a freshly emergent generalized model correcting the pandemic episode and its adverse consequences in multifarious fronts is pursued in this work. Such adverse consequences of pandemic episodes are the incidence of poverty, social insecurity, and unconscionable socioeconomic development in the framework of the loss of moral sustainability.

Indeed, the continuum of sustainability as ethico-economic experience happens by evolutionary learning towards attaining increasing degrees of well-being in the midst of science-economy-society with moral inclusiveness.

Notes

1 On a similar note, Pope Francis addressed in the monthly lecture at the Vatican in the following words: "Please brothers and sisters, let's try to not gossip," he said. "Gossip is a plague worse than COVID. Worse. Let's make a big effort: No gossiping!"
2 See many of the published works of Masudul Alam Choudhury. A most recent one (2019) is entitled *Meta-Science of Tawhid, a Theory of Oneness*, New Palgrave Macmillan, published by Springer Nature, Cham, Switzerland.
3 Arner, D., Avgouleas, E. & Gibson, E. (Aug. 26, 2020). "Financial stability, resolution of systemic banking crises and COVID-19: Toward an appropriate role for public support and bailouts", FinReg Blog, Global Financial Market Center, Duke University School of Law.

Prologue

Prologue 1

O My Lord, increase me in knowledge (*Qur'an*, 20:14)

Prologue 2

If we want students to develop expertise in our fields, then, we have to help them thicken up the connections – from the first week of the semester to the fifth, from the last course they took in our discipline to this one, from the course material to their lives outside of class. The more connections they can create, the more they can begin to formulate their own ideas and gain a wider view of our fields.

> "Small Changes in Teaching: Making Connections 3 Ways that Faculty Members Can Help Students Link Course Content to the World Around Them," *Coping with Coronavirus. The Chronicle of Higher Education.*
> Lan, J.M. (2020)

Our prologues here connect with the content of this entire book in learning how to cope with the wider extant of human pandemic. These comprise coronavirus today and its mutations, and beyond in addressing disabling human predicaments. This feature conveyed in the prologues has been examined in this book and remedies suggested within the multidisciplinary moral inclusive domain of knowledge, consciousness and organization.

1 The socio-scientific development outlook for global future

The project of wellbeing as the multidisciplinary unified model of science-economy-society moral inclusiveness

The wellbeing project of humankind collectively has to struggle uphill; or it will slip downwards in achieving the visionary moral-inclusiveness goal along with its embedding in the mechanistic arm of pedagogy. This holistic goal cannot be reached within a mechanistic approach alone of the socio-scientific understanding of 'value.' The Oneness of God and its explanation in the experiential world-system is the epicenter of the abiding value! Teachers, policymakers, and students must and ought to endeavour to reach the great goal not separately between the mechanistic and the visionary goals oppositely. The discursively derived (interaction) integration (discursive consensus) followed by continuous evolutionary learning in terms of the primal universal ontology of unity of knowledge – thus abbreviated as IIE-learning – forms the philosophy of embedded oneness. This sustained continuity of consciousness in terms of unity of knowledge is the principal way of organic consilience (Wilson, 1998).[1]

The Qur'an refers to this highest echelon of value as monotheistic oneness explainable in the fullest order of reality referred to as Tawhid. Tawhid is the primal ontological law of universal oneness (multidisciplinary ensemble). Upon this ontological primacy of the precept of value Tawhid prevails as the unique and universal law of unity of knowledge transcending shari'ah. Tawhid as law acquires its ultimate epistemic meaning of monotheism as the reality of 'everything' in every way.[2] Islamic scholars for a long time now have failed to understand the ontological meaning, formalism, application, and worldly moral sustainability of Tawhid as law over continuums of unity of knowledge, space (world-system), and time (Al-Raysuni, 2005).[3] This book points out the resilient consequence of deriving the robust theory of consilience as the ultimate value according to Tawhid for the understanding, treatment, cure, and futuristic control of pandemic episode and its adverse consequences as global ecological insecurity (Choudhury & Taifur, 2020).[4]

This work has argued that the philosophy of knowledge and education ought to be different from how they have been pursued in a mechanical context with little or none of the ontological foundation for science-economy-society application within the context of moral inclusiveness. What such knowledge and education now pursue is a mechanistic road map of materiality alone. There is no holistic understanding and practice of vision embedded in techniques.

This study argues and explains analytically the consequences of the belief and practice of the empty mechanistic world-system and worldview. Contrarily, it explains how post-coronavirus pandemic times ought to be a new awakening for all in the world of socio-scientific reality. This new epistemic awakening is expected to be a new vision away from the robotic age of empty mechanism upon which the pandemic episode has ridden rough shod.

Let us ponder over these issues from the two confronting sides!

Post-COVID-19 emergence of epistemic consciousness

Our post-COVID-19 times are also of far-sightedness, creativity, and wise reflections. The resulting vast meanings ought to instil the changed future outlook of academia, education, pedagogy, and global educational policies post-COVID-19. During these cloistered coronavirus global moments at home we have thought about these points. My counterparts as students in Indonesia along with the policymakers of development institutions have joined partnership to ameliorate these dimensions of the new world of learning and knowledge that do and ought to emerge in continuous extension. The search, discovery, and pedagogy along such new dimensions blossomed even in the midst of the sombre burst of coronavirus at the doors of COVID-19 and at the self-conceited genre of our understanding of knowledge and education and the resulting continuation of the enervated world-system. Such is an individuated, mechanistic outlook of the present age devoid of the moral and social values that matter, construct, persist, and sustain life, future. The capitalistic global order with its sparkling splendour of want, greed, and self has fuelled COVID-19 with its unabated rage. We need to enquire deeply in order to reconstruct for a better future and an immediate pandemic control.

Objective

We have commenced by writing on this adoption of the epistemic worldview as a centrepiece of the new order reconstructed via science-economy-society moral inclusiveness. More so its details will encompass the study of the disciplines of business, economics, science, and society with a unique methodological insight for 'everything' so as to be prepared for the pandemic future.

The age of coronavirus and beyond

A definition of novel coronavirus (COVID-19) can be given. Yet the causes of this pandemic have not been identified. The immanence of the virus is not known beyond the knowledge that it emanates in nature in mammals, birds, and respiratory human tracts. This is a limited understanding of the true reality of the strange happening of this disease. Consequently, the return to sustained normalcy out of the deadly chaos has not been found. Any treatment found to temporarily halt the disease has the contrary effect of reducing immunity from imminent diseases.[5] The question to ask is this: What treatments can lead to regain a semblance of healthy state though not the perfect and maximal level of wellbeing?

The objective in such recovery to given states of wellbeing is this: understand, and thereby construct, the awareness and socio-scientific structure of wellbeing as the objective criterion of healthy coexistence. Such objectification of wellbeing must be premised on the methodological understanding of the endemic problem. This stage of knowledge is followed by the derivation of logical formalism to treat the explanation of the endemic problem that the methodology of wellbeing explains. Logical formalism of the structuring of wellbeing and its application by necessary treatments then follows. This experience enhances knowledge of treatments for gaining increasingly sustained levels of wellbeing in all areas. Included in this are control and mitigation of the pandemic episode and of the adverse pandemic effects at large.

Thereby, the emergent remedy of the targeted problem and its treatment towards attaining better semblances of wellbeing is configured by the sequences of inter-causal relations in perpetuity. This process is explained next. The sequence of systemic continuity shown is perpetual. This is thereby sustained over the domains of evolutionary learning, events, time, and sustainability of consciousness. The emergent realms of continuity in the previously mentioned IIE-learning processes convey the essential meaning of sustainability in reducing and controlling the pandemic situation and its adversities. The core determining element in all these processes is the episteme of unity of knowledge as organic complementarities between the good choices at the exclusion and remedying of the bad and unwanted ones. The inherent knowledge-induced comprehension of any and every detail of observation, study, and inference thereby defines the embedding of the morally inclusive multidisciplinary domain of knowledge, knowledge-induced space, and knowledge-induced time.[6] The substantive meaning of sustainability in respect of moral inclusiveness at the avoidance of social exclusion by methodological dissociation is thus the part and parcel of all kinds of problems occurring in the domain of knowledge, knowledge-induced space and time to sustain consciousness by unity of knowledge. That is Tawhid explains organic complementarities between the good choices and avoids the unrecommended ones. Some examples are given next in the light of the IIE-learning properties of the episteme of unity of knowledge.

Example 1

An example of the search for the true reality and its embedded knowledge based on moral inclusiveness at the exclusion of moral decadence is the following representation of multidimensional interaction, integration, and evolutionary learning in truth situation (IIE). The example here is of the effect of interest rate that causes deprivation of ownership and deepening of poverty and inequality. In turn these social malaises are the circular cause and effect of the outburst of the pandemic episode and its adversities.

The moral inclusiveness versus moral exclusiveness effects of increasing and decreasing consciousness, respectively, are explainable by Figure 1.2 as a representation of Figure 1.1.[7]

Worldly experience fully defines the historical opposites of moral inclusiveness and moral exclusion by the completeness of paths like H's. Each point of such historical continua like a,b, . . . is explained by the opposites between moral inclusiveness and moral exclusion. Only

‖Moral Exclusiveness against Moral Inclusiveness in Unconscionable World-System‖

Interest rate⫾	Investment‖	intensification‖ (⫾)	moral exclusiveness‖(⫾)	continuity‖(⫾)
	(self, Individualism)	of 'bad' (pollution, brothels, poverty, inequality, gambling, sickness, unhappiness wants & self, individualism,	(self and other)	in decadence (sustainability⫾(‖))

Figure 1.1 Moral exclusiveness (e.g. interest rate) negating the good in unconscionable world-system

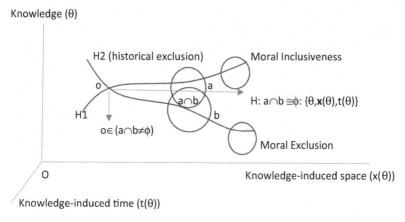

Figure 1.2 Creation and reality in pervasiveness of H: a∩b ≅ φ: {θ,x(θ),t(θ)}

the indefinitely longest path of process learning oppositely between the two realities, described by discretely shown intersecting circles ending up in disjoint circles, defines the eventual path of knowledge-induced points in the productive domain of knowledge, knowledge-induced space, and knowledge-induced time. Such a representation as the perfect straight path is denoted by {θ,x(θ),t(θ)} along H: historical continua, a∩b ≅ φ.

The implication of {θ,x(θ),t(θ)} along H: a∩b ≅ φ is that the meaning of moral inclusiveness by knowledge finds its indispensable presence by embedding in every experiential detail. The meaning of multidisciplinary reality of 'everything' (Barrow, 1991)[8] is thus gained by the properties of interaction, integration, and evolutionary processes of learning between variables defining systems by continua of {θ,x(θ),t(θ)} along H: a∩b ≅ φ. The idea of multidisciplinarity thus negates that of linear addition of disjoint entities without the embedding θ-value in H: {x,t}.

Example 2: quantification of imponderable variable of the wellbeing function

In reference to Figure 1.1, consider the following vector of variables (knowledge-induced space), x(θ) = {interest rate, i; investment, I; nature, N; employment, E; poverty, P; income, Y; endogenous policy by public-private participatory discourse to establish moral inclusiveness contrary to moral exclusion}. The choice of ratios of selected variables can also be the selected variable. In this case, R_i as the following variable explains the relative progress of the moral inclusiveness (moral exclusion). Let $R_1 = (i/I)\downarrow$ as $i\downarrow \Rightarrow I\uparrow$. (N/I) stability, (E/I) stability; $(P/I)\downarrow$; $(E/P)\uparrow$;$(Y/P)\uparrow$. The complementary participative relational advancement in the selected variables is signified by q-induction of all the variables as shown. The R_i-ratios can thus be variously constructed based on the intent of the study on wellbeing of treatment and cure of pandemic in its vastly implied meaning.

Wellbeing

A complete model of wellbeing ($W(\theta)$) and its evaluation followed by empirical policy inferences formulated as logical formalism is given next. This form of the model is just one in many in the family of alternative models that can be constructed according to the intent of the goal and its empirical evaluation (estimation followed by simulation (simulacra)) (Fitzpatrick 2003, Hawking & Mlodinow, 2010).[9] The entire methodological formulation is based on the primal objective of generating positively participatory linkages between the wellbeing enhancing variables of the given vector. Such an inter-relational process is said to be the linkage between endogenous variables. Tawhid as qur'anic law explains the universe in its entirety in terms of such endogenous organic unity of being and becoming (Qur'an, 36:36).[10]

Formulation of the wellbeing function is,

$$\text{Evaluation}_{(\theta)} \, W(\theta) = W(\theta,\mathbf{x}(\theta),t(\theta)); \text{ or, Eval } W(\theta) =$$
$$B(\theta).\Pi_j x_j^{aj}*t^{bj}][\theta_j] \tag{1.1}$$
$$\text{Subject to, } x_k(\theta) = f_k(\mathbf{x}_l(\theta),t(\theta)); (k,l) = 1,2,3,\ldots; k\neq l. \tag{1.2}$$

In respect of the previously mentioned vector of variables, $(\theta,\mathbf{x}(\theta),t(\theta))$, there will be either seven policy-driven selection of endogenous variables; or six endogenous selected variables assuming knowledge induction (policy induction) following their desired trends. Thus, there will be seven or six inter-causal equations in this system corresponding to the sets of vectors of variables given next:

The empirical version of the wellbeing function is,

$$\theta = W(\mathbf{x}(\theta),t(\theta)). \tag{1.3}$$

The estimation and simulation of this derived function (evaluation) points to the empirically measured degree of wellbeing in the entire valuation model.

The generating of θ-values corresponding to $(\mathbf{x}(\theta),t(\theta))$ in time series or survey data is shown later on in this chapter and afterwards.

In the previous case of $\{\theta,\mathbf{x}(\theta),t(\theta)\}$ along the entirety of the given data in H: a$\cap$b $\cong \phi$, a particular case of the $f_k(.\ .)$-equation is this in the two stated cases of the vector of endogenous variables:

$$\log x_k(\theta) = A(\theta) + a_j(\theta)\log(x_l(\theta)) + b(\theta).\log i(\theta); k,l = 1,2,3,4,5, (6); k{\neq}l \tag{1.4}$$

The signs of the dynamic coefficients caused by θ-induction are subject to estimation and revision by simulation. These imply the policy-theoretic effects on the evaluated statistical relations. Following are some examples. Diversely many mathematical forms in the families of equation (1.4) can be used (Suriadi, 2013).[11]

Let $x_k(\theta)$ denote investment (k) caused by endogenous effects of all the other variables on the right-hand-side of equation (1.4). In any particular case, say on the sensitivity study of $x_k(\theta)$ with respect to $i(\theta)$, the estimated value to interpret is the partial elasticity indicator. This value is given by the formula (percentage change in $x_k(\theta)$ with respect to change in θ-value/percentage change in $i(\theta)$ with respect to change in θ-value). This partial inter-variable partial elasticity coefficient is alternatively written as

$$\in_{xk(\theta)/i(\theta)} = [(\partial x_k(\theta)/\partial\theta)/(\partial i(\theta)/\partial\theta)]. \tag{1.5}$$

A statistically significant negative value of $\in_{xk(\theta)/i(\theta)}$ establishes the meaningful relationship of moral inclusiveness between $x_{k(\theta)}$ (investment)↑ and $i(\theta)$ (interest rate)↓ in terms of the respective knowledge-induced regression coefficients. A contrarily weak partial elasticity relationship or other combinations of relations between (investment) and (interest rate) can be interpreted along the path of moral exclusion in Figure 1.1 respective to its intensity.

Similarly all other inter-variable relational interpretations can be made in respect of the paths of moral inclusiveness contrary to moral exclusion by noting the signs of the knowledge-induced regression coefficients as partial elasticity coefficients. In the case of reading the total inter-variable effect

the equation to interpret inter-variable relations by the signs of the knowledge-induced regression coefficients is this:

%change in $x_k(\theta)$ in respect of %change in θ-value = %change in
technological coefficient $A(\theta)$ in respect of %change in θ-value +   (1.6)
$\Sigma_{l=1}^{5(6)}$ [%change in $x_l(\theta)$ in respect of %change in θ-value]

The evaluated trends (estimation followed by simulation) along the paths
of moral inclusiveness contrary to moral exclusion are fully explained by
inferences obtained from equations (1.4)-(1.6) (Choudhury, Al-Muharrami,
S. Ahmed, S., chapter contributed in Choudhury, 2019).[12] The previously
mentioned statistical nature of equations (1.1)-(1.6) and in reference to Figure 1.2 related to Figure 1.1 spans the whole of the historical reality of moral
inclusiveness contrasting with the paths of moral exclusion or reformation
of the latter into nearness to the former.

In the context of including the generalized theory of coronavirus type of
disease by cell-mutation in the vector of interrelated relations mentioned
earlier, particular variables can be noted. For instance, (Nature/Investment)
↑(↓), (Investment/interest rate) ↑(↓), (life-fulfillment/Investment ↑(↓) etc.
can be selected as particular critical variables defining paths of moral inclusiveness contrary to moral exclusion along the perforation of H-paths as
shown in Figure 1.2. Here Nature is equivalent to investment in environment.

The socio-scientific implication of COVID-19 in the general-system
model comprising equations (1.1)-(1.6) and their associated wellbeing
function of knowledge-induced endogenously complementary variables by
interrelations in the ensuing equations can be explained. This is done by
evaluating the imminent multidisciplinary abstracto-empirical phenomenological and evaluative model comprising (1.1)-(1.6).

(Nature/Investment) can be included as the variable for the state of desired
relationship between Investment↑ and its application to increasing Nature↑
projects to establish stability of the relative variable (Nature/Investment)≈↑.
Likewise, (Investment/interest) relative variable is used in the socio-
scientific wellbeing model to explain the decreasing effect of interest rate
on increasing levels of investment in Nature variable. This latter variable is
indicated by increasing (life-fulfillment/Investment) relative variable. The
wellbeing impact is implied in the continua of knowledge, space, and time
dimensions by the induction of θ-value everywhere. The θ-value is determined as empirical measure of consciousness of the variables desired along
the learnt process of recovery to the moral inclusiveness path. Simultaneously also, the endogenous impact of the events of the moral inclusiveness
path on the relative variables etc. is empirically determined in reference to

the methodology of positive complementarity between the endogenous variables of the wellbeing function. Thus θ-value is the underlying determinant of inter-variable causality of moral inclusiveness and of the transformation of social exclusion (disease) into the state of moral inclusiveness (simulated cell renormalization). Such a transformation removes cell mutation by the state of normalcy and by the intermediation of proper treatments.

Finally equations (1.1)-(1.3) processes inter-variable causality by transforming social exclusion to moral inclusiveness by the general-system of equations (1.1)-(1.6). Now by the endogenous impact of organic causality of complementarity between desired choices contrary to the mutation property of oppositeness between the determining variables, the evolutionary process of moral inclusiveness is determined as indicated by Figures 1.1–1.2. The abstracto-empirically evaluated (estimation followed by simulated reconstruction) wellbeing function is denoted by expression (1.1)-(1.3). We write the empirical equation (1.3) of the mathematically abstract expression (1.1) in its empirical form as follows. Pratiwi and colleagues'[13] tabular data used were of the form in Table 1.1. $F(\theta)$ can be estimated in a non-linear functional form by using the data of θ-values in Table 1.1.

The selection of θ-value in Table 1.1 implies degrees of average wellbeing over time according to the socio-scientific variables $x(\theta)$ relative to the best column-value of the particular $\{x_{tj}\}[\theta]$, denoted by $\{x_{tj}*\}[\theta*=10]$. The effectiveness of treatments-specific curative variables are found by evaluation of expressions (1.1)–(1.6) with predictor variables near to $\{x_{tj}*\}[\theta*=10]$. The evaluated wellbeing-values of the increasing returns to scale of $\{\theta*\approx10\}$-values form the moral inclusiveness straight path shown by Figure 1.2.

$$\text{Evaluate } F(\theta) = B(\theta).\Pi_j x_j{}^{aj} * t_j{}^{bj}][\theta_j] \tag{1.7}$$

Table 1.1 Data table of $[\theta, x(\theta), t(\theta)]$ for evaluating the quantitative empirical form (1.7) of the wellbeing function and evaluating the system of equations (1.4)

$t(\theta)$	$x(\theta) = \{x_{tj}\}[\theta]$	$\{\theta_{tj}\}$ = weighted $\theta_{tj} = (x_{tj}/x_{tj}*).$(assigned best value of θ_{tj} corresponding to $x_{tj}* = 10$)	Eval. θ_t
1	$x_{11}(\theta_{11})\ \ x_{12}(\theta_{12})\ldots\ldots.x_{1m}(\theta_{1m})$	$\theta_{11}, \theta_{12}, \ldots, \theta_{1m}$	$Avg_j\theta_{1j}\theta_1$
2	$x_{21}(\theta_{21})\ x_{22}(\theta_{22})\ldots\ldots\ldots x_{2m}(\theta_{2m})$	$\theta_{21}, \theta_{22}, \ldots, \theta_{2m}$	$Avg_j\theta_{2j}\theta_2$
n	$x_{n1}(\theta_{n1})\ \ x_{n2}(\theta_{n2})\ldots\ldots\ldots x_{nm}(\theta_{nm})$	$\theta_{n1}, \theta_{n2}, \ldots, \theta_{nm}$	$Avg_j\theta_{nj}\theta_n$
$t = 1,2,\ldots,n; j = 1,2,\ldots,m$			

Example 3: embedding moral values as curative treatments in mutation of inter-variable relations by return to normalcy

Here is another example showing how to establish the moral embedding value signified by selected socio-economic variables in the quantitative evaluation of the wellbeing function with the endogenous inter-causality between the various socio-economic variables. Of these variables there are those that denote evolutionary process of reducing cellular (organic relations) mutations. An example of such a curative treatment in Islamic belief is to embed worldly functions with true belief in Oneness of Allah, Tawhid as the law of unity of knowledge between all that is good as defined by the monotheistic law. Contrarily all that mutate by opposition to complementarity between the good things are contrary to the Tawhidi law of organic unity of knowledge between the good things of the monotheistic genre.

Increasing moral inclusiveness over moral exclusiveness explained by intensification of faith

We now particularly raise the question how coronavirus pandemic is related with socio-economic variables of the generalized wellbeing system of relations (1.1)-(1.7), which are further embedded and organically related with moral values of monotheistic oneness according to Tawhid as the divine law of oneness. As for the significance of the meanings of faith, belief, and oneness of moral embedding, the compounding of the $\{\theta\}$-knowledge value in the socio-economic variables can be used. Functional compounding proceeds as follows:

$$[\theta, x(\theta), t(\theta)] \rightarrow [\theta(\in 1(\in_2(\in_3(. . . . .); x(\theta(\in_1(\in_2(\in_3(. . . . .)), t(\theta)];$$
t as time series or as survey result. (1.8)

Here $\{\in\}$ denote levels (embedding) of faith within comprehension of unity of knowledge by Tawhid as law. Imam Ghazali (trans. Buchman, 1998)[14] leveled 'j' up to 60 stages. I believe the j-stages form indefinite levels of deepening knowledge and contrarily depths of 'de-knowledge.' The latter state of moral failure embodies worldly (pandemic) and eternal (great pandemic of doomsday) punishment and despondency (Qur'an 14:25–29, Chapter Ibrahim).[15]

$$d\theta(.) = \Sigma_j(\partial\theta(.)/\partial\in_j).(d\in_j) > 0;$$
$$dx_j(\theta(.))/d\theta(.) = \Sigma_j(\partial x_j(\theta_j(.))/\partial\theta_j(.)).(d\theta(.)/d\in_j(.) > 0, \text{ identically by}$$
each term of these expressions (1.9)

Examples of the deeper embedding of θ-values by the attributes of faith, consciousness (taqwa), and moral entities as in (1.8)-(1.9) are conveyed by the conscious attributes of regular prayer by God's remembrance in abidance of the divine law with prescribed practices; cleanliness; sense of establishing social equality by way of charity, choice of financial instruments to enable equality and property rights, blissful communitarianism, etc.[16]

Expression (1.9) can be integrated with the multidisciplinary system of socio-scientific wellbeing criterion given by expressions (1.1)-(1.7) to establish the extended generalized socio-scientific multidisciplinary system of 'everything.' The broadest implication of expression (1.9) regarding embedded multidisciplinarity is that consciousness of goodness conveyed by unity of knowledge between the good choices opposing the mutation nature of social exclusiveness by individuation forms the fundamental ontology of morality, economy, society, and science taken up in multidisciplinary ensemble.

Such interactive, integrative, and evolutionary learning (IIE) worldview of human experience is explained by the paths 'Hs' in Figure 1.2. 'H'-paths are now further detailed by deeper precept of consciousness. The emergent continuum of paths thus describes the entirety of the socio-scientific phenomenological, generalized model of multidisciplinary reality along evolutionary processes of learning. In this regard there are the wise words of Michio Kaku (2015, p. 43):[17] "Consciousness is the process of creating a model of the world using multiple feedback loops in various parameters (e.g. in temperatures, space, time, and in relation to others), in order to accomplish a goal (e.g. find mates, food, shelter)." Kaku calls this definition of phenomenological consciousness as the 'space-time theory of consciousness.'

Tawhidi embedding of unity of knowledge in socio-economic variables

It is important to explain the socio-scientific relevance of Tawhidi law as embedded knowledge in order to understand the organic interrelationship between morality, faith, belief, and the socio-scientific outlook in details. Such importance of organic interrelations has not been understood by the existing scholarly and practitioner community. The result is an utter loss of understanding on the need for a new educational and epistemological worldview in post-coronavirus experience. This worldview will arise as a new integrated conception of analytical multidisciplinarity with methodological foundations premised in the principle of unity of knowledge. The generalized wellbeing model of all unified systems between the good things of life contrary to mutated systems of unwanted things as explained by expressions (1.1)-(1.7) and further extended by expression (1.8) explains the methodological essence of multidisciplinarity in the details of the socio-scientific world-system.

This understanding can be readily found in the case of coronavirus pandemic debacle worldwide in terms of deaths and pestilence, absence of moral consciousness in the education of business, economics, finance, science, society, communitarian behaviour, and institutions by the world-view of moral exclusiveness. The role of constructive religious values as of Tawhidi universality that is embedded in 'everything' integrates the realms of science and faith by organic unity. The substantive meaning of multidisciplinarity is thus born as the permanently sustainable core of embedding of Tawhid as law in 'everything.' The emergent consequence is then represented by the organic complementarity signifying evolutionary process of learning by interaction and integration between the multidisciplinary details of diverse variables and their interrelations via the wellbeing criterion of socio-economic development.

Ignorance of the critical centricity of moral values in curbing socio-scientific disorder

There has been much writing on the topic of health and economic hazards caused by coronavirus pandemic. Yet almost no comprehensive understanding is articulated regarding the role and relationship between religion and the onslaught and cure of COVID-19 across varied fronts. Nonetheless, Allah in Islam as the sustainer of 'everything' by His Tawhidi law exerts a central social role in the overall rise and resolution of the pandemic and its multifarious adversities.

Here is a statement by a conference speaker in the United States during the peak days of coronavirus pandemic as the world was brooding over this global unprecedented catastrophe:[18]

> If all the copies of the Bible were to be thrown into the ocean, the next time no one would know the message of the Bible, for there is no consensus on the messages of the various schools of the Bible. The Bible is not memorized in any standard and unique version. If all the copies of the Qur'an were to be thrown into the sea, so that none remained in earth, the Qur'an can be reproduced word-for-word within the speed of the electronic age. The hafiz (memorizer) of the Qur'an from various different parts of the world, despite their unacquaintance, would recite verbatim, checking on the accuracy of the identical version of the Qur'an.

The Qur'an thus remains the indestructible message of Allah, the monotheistic One, to explain 'everything' in the entire world-system between the heavens and the earth, what is below the earth and above the earth.[19]

I read an article in *The Daily Star* (Bangladesh daily) as a solitary expression on the topic of religion and COVID-19. There was that writer's misunderstanding regarding an incident that explains social ignorance of the Islamic values as moral treatment in curing coronavirus. The event occurred in a 'lift' in Makkah during an Umrah, small pilgrimage. This event coincided with the time of the coronavirus pandemic prior to lockdown. The author wrote about an incident in a lift that was populated by a Saudi family and a Chinese Muslim who was performing his Umrah. The Chinese person sneezed, then felt embarrassed about it. The Saudi family retorted by saying, "La hawla wala quwata illa billah."[20] The author of *Daily Star* took this qur'anic expression to mean exorcism of evil spirit. Contrarily, the real meaning of this qur'anic verse is "there is no power nor ability save by Allah." Such is an example of how Islamic values are misinterpreted and ignored widely.

On the contrary, the correct understanding of Islamic values must invite true reflection on the depth and effectiveness of the all-embracing explanation and practice of such values. They expand across the entirety of human beliefs, lives, and experiential details. The importance of such cardinal values ought to be correctly conveyed to all and in every matter.

In this context we ask: How can Islamic values actualize the return of mutation in pandemic episode to a state of normalcy? Such restoration of normalcy although will not be to a perfect state, yet it can be to an approximated state of wellbeing by progressive stability, having a deep lesson for self and totality of human relations in the experiential world-system.

Islamic monotheistic explanation of the model of converting mutation of cells/viruses into normalcy

This claim is explained in the following way by means of the greatest religious value and which is conveyed irrevocably by the Qur'an. That universal value is known as Tawhid as Law, the Oneness of Allah and its reflection in the experiential world-system explained by the monotheistic sign of oneness. This overarching law is equivalently explained as participatory pairing between the good things of life at the exclusion of or by remedying the unwanted ones. The excluded ones are those that deny the law of organic symbiosis as manifestation of oneness (Qur'an 36:36)[21] in the light of monotheism in belief, formalism, practice, and thus value. This principle also conveys its organic meaning of participative unity in terms of its equivalence to moral inclusiveness in the order and scheme of all good things while avoiding the contrary ones absolutely or relatively along the sustainable path of science-economy-society model of moral inclusiveness.

The pairing principle of monotheistic oneness implies organic interrelations between diversity of the multidisciplinary order and scheme of all things. In the case of COVID-19, this disease is embedded in cellular mutation as chaos caused by the vastness of virus proliferation. Renormalization by the law of oneness implies application of treatments that bring back the vastly mutated COVID-19 cells out of chaos and reforms them in the nature and structure of organic oneness as normalcy in the good things, practices, and value. Thereby, the renormalized unified diversity replaces the mutated cells. Mutated cellular viruses contrarily deny the oneness of renormalization. The latter type of reality shows abidance of the world-system to the monotheistic law ontologically as response to the equivalence of such chaos in moral exclusiveness that imitate experiences in science, economy, and society at large. Yet these adoptions of the ethical types ignore the worthy behaviourism and consciousness of the fullness of moral inclusiveness.

Thus, the domain of multidisciplinary inclusiveness foundationally exists by way of the primal existence of monotheistic oneness – Tawhid as law. This law regenerates consistency, continuity, and sustainability in precept, practice, and value. All such attributes unified together in abstraction and practice form the dynamics of the entire worldview of renormalization by unity of knowledge as the principle of oneness and as the pervasive functioning of the monotheistic signs in the order of 'everything' as we understand this conception by the monotheistic ontology of unity of knowledge.

Economic devastation is pandemic consequences marked by enormous increase in unemployment, long-term disability to recover from global economic slump in production, trade, national economic growth, and development plans. Such debilities are especially prevalent in developing countries. Above all, the cessation of sustainability in social policy and public plans on expansion and investment have joined together as multidimensional system cells of disarray. Such pandemic despoil is marked by mutation, death, and decadence both on the human side and in environment, economy, and society.

Such abnormal states imitate the chaos of mutation, which in human behaviour is reflected in methodological individualism of economic and social behaviour. Likewise, the dissociation between opposing economic and social entities that represent mutated cells as of pandemic episodes needs to be remedied by treatment. Mutation in all these kinds must be reversed to normalcy by the discovery and application of holistic treatment, control, and cure. The result is one of unifying the good and realizing unity of the good effects into a coherent effectiveness of normalization via treatment and recovery. The multidimensional model of unity of knowledge in such a case is premised in the epistemic premise of unity of knowledge prevailing in science-economy-society model of moral inclusiveness.

Reversing cellular/coronavirus mutation into normalcy of unity of healthy cells

The primal religious message that applies to the curative design of renormalization out of mutated cellular multidimensional chaos is characterized in and attained by the model of moral inclusiveness premised in unity of knowledge. This means dissociation of socially exclusive elements contrary to unifying between the good choices of moral inclusiveness. The curative transformation here reflects unity of knowledge of the renormalized cells. Thereby comes about the cessation of pandemic chaos of mutation and the realization of the curative role of Islam, knowledge, faith, and the details of the world-system.

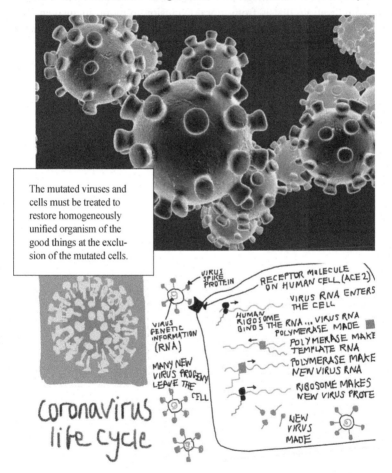

The mutated viruses and cells must be treated to restore homogeneously unified organism of the good things at the exclusion of the mutated cells.

Figure 1.3 Isolating cellular (viral) mutation of COVID-19 by treatment to restore normalcy of cells

Coronavirus peak and flattening curves with and without induction by unity of knowledge

Figure 1.4 is the curve of prediction of the peak, P, which then declines to a flattening F of the mutation of COVID-19 over a period of time. The differences in shape, form, and interpretation of COVID-19 life between Figure 1.1 and Figure 1.4 are shown by the non-learning and non-dynamic nature of the latter contrasting with the knowledge-induction of unity of knowledge that transforms mutation into renormalization of cells. Such a transformation is indicated in Figure 1.4. The evolutionary learning property of interaction and integration towards transformation from mutation to renormalization, that is from moral exclusion to moral inclusiveness is a knowledge-induced process of sustainability across continuum. That is events appear and disappear in the continuum of knowledge, space, and time dimensions. All events are induced by and understood within the impact of the episteme of unity of knowledge. Such dynamics of change occur thereby in the knowledge, knowledge-induced space, and knowledge-induced time dimensions. The result is a different process than that in Figure 1.1. Figure 1.4 shows the sheer time-dynamics of change between peak and flattening of COVID-19 episode. The concept of sustainability is explained in Figure 1.2 as a long-term reconstruction of mutation into normalcy by

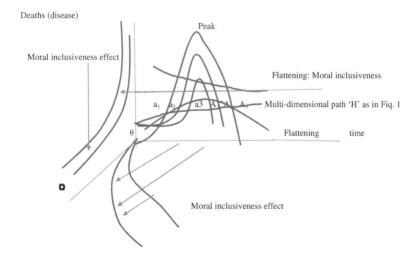

Figure 1.4 Equivalence between peak-flattening curve and moral inclusiveness in case of disease (coronavirus)

adoption of moral inclusiveness by multidisciplinary embedding. The transformation process into moral inclusiveness is explained by Figure 1.4.

Despite the cross-sectional view of the coronavirus peak and flattening curve in time and deaths (disease), the projection of the improving points like a, b, c etc. on the decline of deaths by the moral learning effects over time is enhanced. This is the picture conveyed by Figure 1.1 as well, with the inclusion of $\{\theta(\varepsilon),x(\theta(\varepsilon)),t(\theta(\varepsilon))\}$-values (Choudhury, 2019).[22]

Conclusion

This chapter has invoked awareness in teaching, researching, and learning by deep thinking in our times of unprecedented adversities so as to discover new ways regarding the world between self and other. The new age of post-coronavirus times in particular and the excruciating problems in general caused by moral exclusion must fill up the new paraphernalia of the philosophy of knowledge and education with the moral impression and by casting off the dissociative separation in moral exclusion.

Our existing textbooks and curricula do not instil the teachers and the students with the overarching moral and material relevance of the details of the world-system. Teachers, students, policymakers, and textbooks are not prepared and trained to uphold the big picture, instead of the narrow perspective of a morally exclusive philosophy of education, knowledge, and the consequential social disorder. Thus, we as teachers, students, and the rest in the futile knowledge domain have failed in every aspect of teaching, practicing, and sustaining the emergent lesson of moral inclusiveness. We as teachers in our present state of emptiness of education and knowing impart through the empty pursuit of a general wellbeing by discovering this in the world of mechanistic materiality with technicalities separated from the epistemic fullness of understanding and by practicing the reality of unifying self with other in soul, mind, and matter.

It is therefore time now to bestow the full scope of knowledge and education contrary to the moral exclusion of these fields from simply the individualistic worldview of mechanistic technicalities serving self without the holistic other. The emergent dreary prospect of methodological individualism of the entire social order would then forever pave the way to an empty capitalist world of moral and social exclusion (Pickety, 2017).[23] It is most urgent now to reconstruct the socio-scientific order of moral inclusiveness with self and other in an interactive, integrated, and evolutionary world-system. The emergent model of science-economy-society moral inclusiveness would then overarch between the study and control of pandemic episode and its adverse episodic consequences at large to a better future.

Notes

1 Wilson, E.O. (1998). *Consilience, the Unity of Knowledge*, Vantage Books, New York, NY.
2 Qur'an (69:1–3): "The Inevitable Reality – What is the Inevitable Reality? And what can make you know what is the Inevitable Reality?"
3 Al-Raysuni, A. (2005). *Imam Al-Shatibi's Theory of the Higher Objectives and Intents of Islamic Law*, International Institute of Islamic Thought, Herndon, VA.
4 Choudhury, M.A. & Taifur, M.A. (2020). "Consilience as Islamic methodology of Tawhid: The general socio-scientific framework", in N. Maghrebi, T. Akin, A. Mirakhor & A. Iqbal, eds. *Handbook of Analytical Studies in Islamic Finance and Economics*, pp. 29–52, Walter de Gruyter, Berlin, Germany.
5 "Coronavirus", from Wikipedia, https://en.wikipedia.org/wiki/Coronavirus, visited March 29, 2020.
6 Qur'an (7:54) on the precedence of Tawhid over time and creation: "Allah created the heavens and the earth, and all that is between them, in six days" (7:54).
7 The need for explaining the underlying idea leads to the use of Cartesian geometrical frame. Essentially, all analysis in respect of Figure 1.2 in Tawhidi worldview is conducted by non-Cartesian algebraic approach. A case of this approach is mathematical topology (Maddox, 1970). *Elements of Functional Analysis*, Cambridge University Press, Cambridge.
8 Barrow, J.D. (1991). *Theories of Everything, the Quest for Ultimate Explanation*, Oxford University Press, Oxford.
9 Fitzpatrick, T. (2003). "Postmodernism and new directions", in P. Alcock, A. Erskine & M. May, eds. *Social Policy*, pp. 125–133, Blackwell, Oxford.
     Hawking, S.W. & Mlodinow, L. (2010). *The Grand Design*, Transworld Publishers, London.
10 Qur'an (36:36): "Exalted is He who created all pairs – from what the earth grows and from themselves and from that which they do not know".
11 Suriadi, J. (2013). "Factors influencing proportionate numbers of micro-entrepreneurs in Indonesia", unpublished Ph.D. dissertation, Postgraduate Program in Islamic Economics and Finance, Trisakti University, Jakarta, Indonesia.
12 Choudhury, M.A., Ahmed, S. & Al-Muharrami, S. (2018). *Tawhidi Methodological Worldview (Islamic Economics as Transdisciplinary Study)*, Springer Nature.
13 Pratiwi, A., Choudhury, M.A. & Ismal, R. (2017). *The Islamic Bank's New Paradigm, Challenges and Blessing*, Noor Publishing, Deutschland, Germany.
14 Ghazali trans. Buchman (1998). "God has seventy veils of light and darkness; were He to lift them, the august glories of His face would burn up everyone whose eyesight perceived Him". This quotation is from
     Buchman, D., trans. (1998). *Al-Ghazali Niche of Lights*, Brigham University Press, Provo, Utah.
15 Qur'an (14:25–29): Have you not considered how Allah presents an example, [making] a good word like a good tree, whose root is firmly fixed and its branches [high] in the sky? It produces its fruit all the time, by permission of its Lord. And Allah presents examples for the people that perhaps they will be reminded. And the example of a bad word is like a bad tree, uprooted from the surface of the earth, not having any stability. Allah keeps firm those who believe, with the firm word, in worldly life and in the Hereafter. And Allah sends astray the wrongdoers. And Allah does what He wills. Have you not considered those

who exchanged the favor of Allah for disbelief and settled their people [in] the home of ruin? [It is] Hell, which they will [enter to] burn, and wretched is the settlement.

16 Qur'an (5:6): "Allah does not intend to inconvenience you, but He intends to purify you and perfect His favor to you, so that you may give thanks."

Qur'an (2:43): "And be steadfast in prayer; practise regular charity; and bow down your heads with those who bow down (in worship)."

17 Kaku, M. (2015). "Consciousness–a physicist's viewpoint", in his *The Future of the Mind*, Chapter 2, Anchor Book, New York, NY.

18 VID 2020031-WA0001 (2).

19 Qur'an (65:12). "God is he who created seven heavens (And of the earth their like) The command descending between them That you might know that God is powerful over all things; and that God has encompassed all things in knowledge."

20 Qur'an (18:39): "There is no power nor ability save by Allah."

21 Qur'an (36:36). "Exalted is He who created all pairs – from what the earth grows and from themselves and from that which they do not know."

22 Choudhury, M.A. (2019). *Tawhidi Methodological Worldview (Islamic Economics as Transdisciplinary Study)*, Springer Nature.

23 Pickety, T., trans. & Goldhammer, A. (2017). *Capital in the Twenty-First Century*, Belknap Press of Harvard University Press, Boston, MA.

2 Pandemic treatments for transforming cell mutation into normalcy in unity of knowledge as the ontological premise of technical modelling

Introduction

The ever-evolutionary learning universe of 'everything' (Barrow, 1991)[1] in the framework of abstracto-empirical modulation of unity of knowledge as the primal ontological premise is followed thereby by a plethora of diverse functional ontologies (Gruber, 1993; Maxwell, 1962).[2] Such secondary ontologies convey the diversity of models and structures of logical formalism in the multidisciplinary context. Now in reference to Chapter 1 the context of mutation of coronavirus is one logical form that emanates from the ontology of oppositeness to unity of knowledge that characterizes the nature of methodological individualism. Thereby, the continuity of such mutations in the *res extensa* domain of its own persistence marks its own contrary form of continuum to the case of continuity of normalcy. Normalcy is the continuous unified state or paired by organic unity of knowledge that complements in the realm of knowledge, space, and time in contrariness to mutations as disjoint and thereby discontinuous entities. Yet by the intervention of appropriate treatments of the socio-scientific nature reversals are possible. That is mutations in their states of methodological individualism ('de-knowledge') can reconstruct into organic pairing by unity of knowledge arising from the learnt ontology of complementary oneness. Mutations thereby reconstruct into normalcy by the application of treatments that manifest the abstracto-empirical nature of unity of knowledge. On the other hand, normalcy can deconstruct into mutations. Improper treatments could be a cause of such socio-scientific degradation. The treatments are flawed by their application of separateness in the dissociative multidisciplinary worldview of 'de-knowledge.'

An example of reconstruction of mutations into normalcy out of the state of coronavirus is to discover treatments that organically pair. That is such treatments complement between materiality and the moral and ethical inclusiveness in the socio-scientific holism in the context of unifying these domains by the application of the methodology of unity of knowledge. The search for a vaccine based purely on medical science at the expense of behavioural change with psychological attitude towards wellbeing and moral inclusiveness in the global social order at large would be a fiasco in terms of sustainability. In that case, only local cure with vaccine may be possible. Coronavirus in its vastly mutated form will subsequently arise and continue. Vaccine and medical treatments will thus fail to be a sustainable actualization in wellbeing. The global order will forever remain divided in its search for a unified outlook in wellbeing and sustainability. Capitalism will prevail as the sickness of a methodological individualized world competing for self, power, and hegemony. The resulting human world-system will thus be corrupted by capitalism or another (Pickety, 2017; Wallerstein, 1980).[3]

Towards abstracto-empirical innovation of multidisciplinary ensemble according to the ontology of unity of knowledge and the particularities of diversity in the world-system

Such an inept approach to treatment of coronavirus pandemic is found with the American political and power struggle that had overridden the prolonged contest between the US government and the states on the matter of lockdown against reopening the economy for these two opposing forms of wellbeing. The souring geopolitical factor showed up by the opposing relations between the American and Chinese versions concerning the laboratory origin of coronavirus virus.

The contrasting treatments approach on arresting the advance of coronavirus was also noted in the almost exclusive focus that was placed on technological solution to the pandemic at the negligence of a behavioural socio-psychological approach. This was the type of treatment that was supported by Bill Gates in spite of his most charitable viewpoint on spending in various elements of social wellbeing that Bill Gates upholds (UTube, TED Talk, "The next outbreak").

We will argue using the multidisciplinary unified ontological formalism, that to attain such a socio-scientific objective goal requires the methodology of stabilizing sustainability as inter-causal experience in diversity arising from unity of knowledge by interaction, integration, and evolutionary (IIE) learning. The embedded uncertainty of attaining full effectiveness of treatment will always remain. Hence it is futile to aim at discovering a perfectly functioning vaccine, antibody test, and merely alternative means of cure. The probabilistic nature of pandemic will prevail. Yet lowering this incidence ought to be the advancing objective of abstracto-empirical innovations arising from the embedding between technology and psycho-behavioural span of investigation within the socio-scientific ontology of unity of knowledge across knowledge, space, and time dimensions.

Not a religious mendicant treatment for pandemic episode

It is pursued among the religiously motivated that pandemic, which is caused by the will and law of the Almighty, would ultimately be resolved to containment by God's Will. Therefore, it is observed by the religiously motivated that deepening supplication to God Almighty and increased commitment to religious rites will ultimately revert the calamity to its resolution by God's Will. While this conviction among the religiously motivated may be true, the approach and the resulting treatment by prayer principally is another extreme case of incorrectly understanding the divine law in the absence of the organic ontological principle of unity of knowledge (Qur'an, 36:36). Thereby, such an isolated understanding of the completed universe of wellbeing in complementarity between science and religion is a fiasco of the correct ontological law of unity of knowledge in relation to the wellbeing and sustainability with the world-system. Religion, faith, and belief become empty constructs in such a form of individualism. The result then is yet a similar form of mutation of misguided moral and ethical induction of scientific experience. Religion and science and thereby the entire framework of discovering the knowledge and complementary interrelations between science and religion remain void and meaningless. Such a superstitious and empty invoking of faith and belief isolated from science and vice versa has proved the cause of several adverse coronavirus consequences by way of religious gatherings in Pakistan under the false knowledge of Islamic belief. Jamat-Islami open air convocation in Pakistan in the false pretext of religious orthodoxy while ignoring social distancing and face masking caused a large spike in coronavirus incidence in Pakistan then.

Yet it has proved to be equally damaging of Islamic belief, practice, and understanding of the Islamic faith and its relationship with the nature and structure of the world-system that the ontological law of divine oneness as unity of knowledge bears on Islamic sustainability of complementarity between science and religion. The contrary view of science, technology, and religion can be read off Stephen Hawking's quote (1988, pp. 10–11):

> The eventual goal of science is to provide a single theory that describes the whole universe. However, the approach most scientists actually follow is to separate the problem into two parts. First, there are the laws that will tell us how the universe changes with time. . . . Second, there is the question of the initial state of the universe. Some people feel that

science should be concerned with only the first part; they regard the question of the initial situation as a matter for metaphysics or religion. They would say that God, being omnipotent, could have started the universe off any way he wanted. That may be so, but in that case, he also could have made it develop in a completely arbitrary way. Yet it appears that he chose to make it evolve in a very regular way according to certain laws. It therefore seems equally reasonable to suppose that there are also laws governing the initial state.

This quote summarizes the status of the interrelationship between God, soul, mind, and matter as an organic holism in meaningful socio-scientific fronts.

First, there is the recognition of the uniquely scientific status of the principle of epistemic unity of a single theory that describes the whole universe. In the abstracto-empirical foundation of multidisciplinary methodological worldview the single theory would represent the ontological premise of unity of knowledge. In qur'anic methodological worldview the ontological premise of unity of knowledge is derived from the principle of multidisciplinary pairing (complementing) as relations between the good things of life in their diversities of being; and the avoidance of the episteme of utilitarian methodological individualism (Quinton, 1989)[4] resulting in mutation of the corresponding unwanted diversities in shape, form, and applications of self and other.

Second, the Hawking quote points to the contradictory nature of scientific thinking of the old genre. This approach is categorized as separating the problem into two opposing parts. This is a form of methodological individualism that represents the feigned socio-scientific oppositeness between moral inclusiveness and scientific and technological exclusiveness. In the coronavirus treatment for normalcy as unified organism by complementarities between the moral, social, and scientific choices the other categorical part of science and technologically exclusivity forms mutated socio-scientific opposites. Effective treatment of coronavirus then fails.

The third part of the Hawking quote points to the absence of the dynamic and phenomenological functioning in an outlandish nature of idle surrender to the divine law: "He (God) chose to make it (the universe) evolve in a very regular way according to certain laws." The universal and unique law of unity of knowledge with its ontological formalism and phenomenological application in continuum of knowledge, space, and time domain forms the dynamic organic constitution of the qur'anic law of monotheistic oneness. It is explained by the ontological functioning of unity of knowledge.

Einstein remarked that God does not play dice. That is a personal God cannot explain the ultimate intricacies of creation, as in the extensive probabilistic nature of entire creation as framed by Heisenberg's probabilistic principle of uncertainty. Rather, as we formulate the ontological explanation of the functioning of the divine law there is a clear premise, formalism, explanation, and functioning towards attaining truth in the divine law. This actualization being universal and unique across the domain of 'everything' the divine law exists in cosmic reality. But beyond Einstein the microcosm of self is embedded in the divine macrocosm of 'everything.' The fact that the divine monotheistic law is the universal and unique law of oneness, premised in the organistic world-system of complementary pairing between good choices, and contrary to the 'de-knowledge' of mutative methodological individualism, establishes the ontological, dynamic, and functioning nature of complementary pairing according to the divine law of oneness in terms of explaining the episteme of unity of knowledge.

The origin of coronavirus according to the ontological law of unity of knowledge

When the ontological law of unity of knowledge and its contrariety, the mutation theory of 'de-knowledge' (Fischetti & Krzywinski, June 2020)[5] are applied to explain the origin of coronavirus, the distinctive 'treatment' question emerges. The articulation of this primal issue generalizes into a theory of health versus disease. This is equivalent to formulating an analytical study of normalcy versus mutation as the abstracto-empirical comprehensive theory of wellbeing on the sustainability scale.

Some examples of such complemented organic treatment to normalcy and wellbeing by the approach of the ontology of unity of knowledge can be provided, leaving more detailed study of such examples to a later chapter. Take the example of Prophet Muhammad's medicine (Ibn Qayyim al-Jauziyah, transl. Johnston, 1998).[6] This publisher writes regarding the Prophet's medicine in the following words:

> (It) is a combination of religious and medical information, providing advice and guidance on the two aims of medicine – the preservation and restoration of health – in careful conformity with the teachings of Islam as enshrined in the Qur'an and the *hadith*, or sayings of the Prophet.

This translated book is a profound compendium of natural medicine for ailments of all kinds and at all stages of intensification of ailment. In modern times the treatments given in the Prophet's text can be further advanced and refined with the combination of technological change and scientific and medicinal innovations and made available to all as regular medicinal supplements.

Ingredients of Prophet Muhammad's medicinal prescription comprise among other herbal groups, honey, blackseed, azwa dates, chicory (hindaba), figs, olives, garlic, ginger, onions, lentils, and many others (Qur'an, 2:262).[7] Even today these can be found in their rarity in the hilly market of Uhud in Madinah. The principle of integrated medicine and regular curative according to Prophet's recommendation and practice would be to use the main ingredients to complement with the diversity of edible and health-researched wellness by natural sources. To these medicinal offspring modern scientific, technological, and medical elements of innovation can be applied. In all such advancements it would be centrally important to preserve the groundwork and orientation of unity of knowledge (Tawhid) as primal ontology at the level of ontological formalism and its abstracto-empirical processes of sustained application. The totality of such abstracto-empirical understanding and advancement of the Prophet's medicine on a sustained scale forms the endogenous interface by inter-causal relations between the socio-scientific principles of Islamic faith, cleanliness, and artefacts.

Wellbeing effect of integrated medicine

A brilliant example of such wellbeing outcome on a sustained complemented faith and commercial development is the case of Hamdard as an international corporation based on and advanced by integrating morality and ethical standards with progressive medical science. Hamdard has human resource development components, laboratory implementations, and technological innovation features underlying its popularity among many. In its own published legendary terms:

> Hamdard is an institution of Eastern System of Medicine dedicated for health care, and education and a movement for the promotion of morality, science and culture. Hamdard benefits from the accumulated knowledge of centuries, blends it with the latest scientific technology and converts it into efficacious herbal medicine to cure the sufferings of mankind all over the world.

Sustainability effectiveness along with wellbeing and advancement of the Prophet's Medicine at the Hamdard type institutional and commercial level is centrally based on the derived principle of unity of relations. This phenomenon as a socio-scientific creativity is explained and applied by recursively formed complementary extension with cause and effect between diverse number of possibilities. The prevailing mainstream socio-scientific abidance by substituting one good or bad elements of development by another is replaced by possibilities arising from organic unity between the good things. The same ontological foundation of unity of knowledge gained through the evolutionary learning process of interaction between variables leading to integration in states of evolutionary learning equilibriums (Choudhury, 2012)[8] applies to avoidance and progressive reduction of all complementary 'bad.' The meanings of 'good' and 'bad' are similar to those of 'truth' and 'false,' respectively. They arise from the intensifying wellbeing and sustainability concept and their contrariness, respectively.

In the context of the foundational principle of unity of knowledge as of complementing by inter-causal relations between the 'good' variables of medical science and technology and those of morality and moral inclusiveness, this phenomenology can be summarized as follows. Details of brief formalism are left for a later chapter. Parts of it emanating from the ontological law of unity of knowledge and taking its shape, form, application, and meaning with regard to 'everything' can be retrieved from Chapter 1. The particularity of coronavirus pandemic as 'de-knowledge' and its treatment in the formalism of unity of knowledge can thus be studied.

Embedded vector/matrix/tensor variables: (i) consciousness $\{\varepsilon\}$; (ii) knowledge $\{\theta(\varepsilon)\}$; (iii) artefact $\{X(\theta(\varepsilon))\}$ (iv) time $\{t(X(\theta(\varepsilon))\}$. All this comprise the domain of knowledge, space, and time for the study of the wellbeing and sustainability of normalcy in COVID-19 episode by unity of knowledge moral and moral inclusiveness of science, technology, and medicine.

$\Rightarrow Z(\theta(\varepsilon))=\{\theta(\varepsilon), X(\theta(\varepsilon)), t(X(\theta(\varepsilon))\}$ This is the vector/matrix/ tensor representation knowledge and knowledge-induced space-time dimension.

$\Rightarrow$ wellbeing objective criterion in with inter-causal relations between $Z(\theta(\varepsilon))$: $W(Z(\theta(\varepsilon))$, s.t. inter-relations between $Z(\theta(\varepsilon))$; and $\theta(\varepsilon) = W(Z(\theta(e))$

$\Rightarrow$ continuity sustainability: simulacra of coefficients of wellbeing estimation by algorithm and discourse of the knowledge-based society.

Properties of the ontological functions: $[dW(Z(\theta(\varepsilon))/d(\theta(\varepsilon))].(d(\theta(\varepsilon))/d\varepsilon] > 0$, in the extended differential form. This form is true for both consciously based knowledge-induction and for 'de-knowledge' with the particularity of 'truth' versus 'falsehood' choices, respectively.   (2.1)

The phenomenological evaluation of knowledge-induced and contrarily 'de-knowledge'-induced objective criteria, as between normalcy in the framework of unity of knowledge and methodological individualism in pandemic mutation, establishes the universal model of all states of the world-system. A wider sense of such a categorization invokes both the mainstream socio-scientific theory of marginal substitution (neoclassicism and social Darwinism) and the ontological law of extensive complementarities signifying the universal principle of unity of knowledge (Daly et al., 1992).[9] The ontological methodology of Tawhidi unity of knowledge explains 'everything' in the generality and particulars of the diverse world-systems. On the contrary, no other methodological worldview is capable of explaining the phenomenology of Tawhidi unity of knowledge. Thereby, on the curative treatment of pandemic in general the Tawhidi law universalizes by integrating the Tawhidi moral inclusiveness into scientific and technological holism. By the same accord the continuum of complementary relationship between wellbeing and sustainability is established by Tawhidi methodological worldview of unity of knowledge. This is denied by any other methodological phenomenology of reality because of the continuum prevalence of methodological individualism that represents the core of pandemic mutation contrary to the principle of normalcy.

Figure 2.1 is equivalent to the generalized nature of dilution by treatment (RCT) using the modelled approach of Tawhidi unity of knowledge shown in Figure 1.2. The important inference is to point out what is indicated in Figure 1.2 by way of treatment affecting mutation by its break-up into a normalcy cluster of cells, thus converting them into a mutation-free domain of

Heightened cell mutation as Evolutionary 'de-learning':
$(d/d\theta_1)[\cup\cap f_1(\theta_1,x_1(\theta_1),t(\theta_1))]>0\uparrow$
Incorrect RCT, $\{x_1(\theta_1)\}$

Heightened normalcy by evolutionary unity of knowledge using treatments $(x_2(\theta_2))$ of cell destruction:
$(d/d\theta_2)[\cup\cap f_2(\theta_2,x_2(\theta_1),t(\theta_2))]>0\uparrow$

Reconstructive pandemic process and vice-a-versa
$(d\theta_2/d\theta_1)[f(\cup\cap(f_1,f_2)(\theta_1,\theta_2,x_1(\theta_1),x_2(\theta_2),t_1(\theta_1),t_2(\theta_2))]$
$\longrightarrow$ evolutionary learning
$\longleftarrow$

evolutionary mutation (de-learning)
$\cup$ is operational over numbered interaction
$\cap$ is operational over numbered integration
as evolutionary learning (de-learning) proceeds
in knowledge, space, time (likewise for de-learning).
according to the property of differentiable continuity
as functions operate continuously.   (2.2)

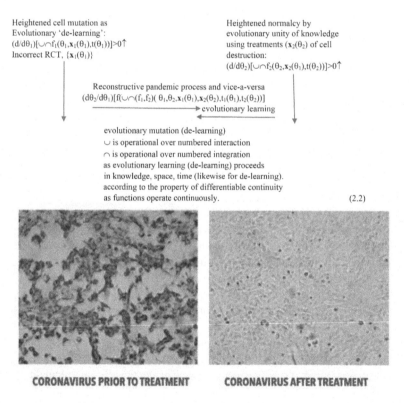

CORONAVIRUS PRIOR TO TREATMENT   CORONAVIRUS AFTER TREATMENT

Figure 2.1 Laboratory-generated dilution of mutated coronavirus into normalcy by RCT treatments

normalcy. Regarding the previous discussion on organically unified moral inclusiveness contrary to the otherwise exclusive medicinal treatments, the progressive evolutionary learning causes a deeper impact on wellbeing. Such a continuity of wellbeing is signified by positive complementarities between the good things of life and their organically knowledge-induced sustainability in continuum.

Staying in lockdown for 14 days, frequently washing hands with soap and sanitizer and taking frequent baths to remain clean, and practising social distancing and face masks are 'good' behavioural habits of mind, body, and consciousness. Along with these include prayers and clean habits in our daily lives as recommended by medical science and moral inclusiveness. In post-coronavirus episode the moral and global cooperation for the common wellbeing and its sustainability combine together to alleviate social, economic, and scientific ills.

Such an integrated sustainable wellbeing is pursued by the World Health Organization in the following words of its commitment: WHO addresses government health policy with two aims:[10] first, "to address the underlying social and economic determinants of health through policies and programmes that enhance health equity and integrate pro-poor, gender-responsive, and human rights-based approaches"; and second, "to promote a healthier environment, intensify primary prevention, and influence public policies in all sectors so as to address the root causes of environmental threats to health." WHO prescription is a semblance of the complementary embedding between science, economy, society, and technology model of moral inclusiveness. In some respects this kind of interactive and integral view of socio-scientific evolutionary learning prevails within the ontology of unity of knowledge. This is our prescriptive formal modelling for studying the coronavirus transformation away from mutation in the social world and contrarily as mutation of cells in deepening sickness. The same model of moral inclusiveness with its episteme applies uniquely as the way of transformation into normalcy by unity of knowledge of effective socio-scientific treatments. Figure 2.1 depicts such a transformation away from viral mutation into normalization by unifying the cells into normal cell reconstruction.

The conglomerates of diverse herbs, fruits, and vegetables as noted down in the Qur'an (2:261), mentioned earlier, also implies the unification as organic embedding between the good things of life, including multidisciplinary learning, interface of moral, scientific, and technological artefacts, and across and within such diversities of useful treatments. Thereby, systems of treatments arise that can be used in organically complementary combinations. In the modelled version of unity of knowledge a large-scale computerized system of wellbeing objective goal arises. Such a model can be the reference to the transformation finalization shown in Figure 2.1.

Model symbolism and treatment for restoring mutation to normalcy with unity of knowledge

The sudden eruption of coronavirus as one example of a great pandemic has failed to unravel its cause and origin. Viruses in general are invisible organisms. They owe their mutation and its destruction towards normalcy to yet unknown explained treatments. Thus, by its reformation, normalcy attained from an episode of viral mutation will always exist as an invisible curative and investigated organism. In the episteme of unity of knowledge the methodological worldview of treatment conveyed by Figure 2.1 is a symbolic study of mathematical consequences as are explained by expression (2.1). The meaning conveyed here is that complementary applications of treatments as RCTs exemplified in Chapter 1 with the ontological model of unity of knowledge configure possible complementarities in the health versus illness scenario. Such a model deepens the associated wellbeing with moral sustainability for a long duration in knowledge, space, and time knowledge-induced continuum. These are the fundamental ingredients of the universal methodological model of unity of knowledge applied to verities of the health versus illness scenarios and treatments. Such verities of problems and their treatments in the mathematical model of unity of knowledge as logical formalism convey the importance of psychological behaviour through its practice and enforcement by the application of knowledge as ontological treatment with the attributes of conviction of belief, behaviour, psychology, policies, and moral choices at large.

There is now the following conclusion regarding our prescriptive model. The ontological methodological worldview of unity of knowledge forms the prescribed premise of an analytical model of socio-scientific nature of cure. This model is simulated by an evaluation of the wellbeing objective criterion in the continuum of sustainability. In the new awakening era of pandemic treatment and avoidance to a large scale in evolutionary processes of model simulation, science and technology, research and development, government, industry, the global institutional order, and policy applications could be preparatory instruments. This approach is a comprehensive one that Bill Gates in spite of his foreboding on the coming age of pandemic episode forgot to encapsulate within a moral and material wrapping as of embedding the model with the episteme of unity of knowledge (Bill Gates, 2015–04–03). "The next outbreak? We are not ready," U- Tube, TED).

A pandemic example: formulating the wellbeing objective criterion

A wellbeing function can be formulated for pandemic case by considering [(health variables)/(illness variables)] ratio in terms of their vector form as presented in Chapter 1. Health and illness variables in such a ratio move oppositely. On the other hand, the positive relationship of the ratio-variable in the wellbeing objective criterion to examine the impact of multidisciplinary premises of treatments could be the ratio-variables as those pertaining to [(health variables)/(wellness variables)]. Many such variables can be tried out to simulate the effectiveness of treatments in the assigned wellbeing function of inter-variable complementarities in the underlying multidisciplinary integral framework. With all the aforementioned symbolic definitions, the wellbeing objective function in its non-linear complex form exemplifying the properties of endogenous circular causal relations between complementary variables can be written down as follows:

$$W(\mathbf{Z}(\theta(\varepsilon))) = \text{either in the case of S-unified system:}$$
$$W_s(\mathbf{Z}(\theta(\varepsilon))) = \Pi_{i=1}{}^n A(\theta(\varepsilon)).X_i(\theta(\varepsilon))^{k_i(\theta(\varepsilon))} \qquad (2.3)$$
$$\text{or in } S_j(\mathbf{Z}_j(\theta(\varepsilon))) \text{ systemic form as,}$$
$$\Pi_j S_j(S_j(\mathbf{Z}_j(\theta(\varepsilon)))) = \Pi_j[\Pi_{i=1}{}^n A(\theta(\varepsilon)).X_i(\theta(\varepsilon))^{k_i(\theta(\varepsilon))}]_{Sj}$$

The wellbeing function as the evaluative objective function of unity of knowledge in multivariate and multidisciplinary sense can be formulated in various selected forms pertaining to the diverse problems at hand. All such wellbeing functions maintain the same mathematical property. They must all be evaluated subject to the entire system of endogenously interrelated inter-variable circular causation equations. This feature was shown in Chapter 1. It is represented in expression (2.3).

In the second case, the interaction, integration, and evolutionary learning dynamics by simulation of the wellbeing function imply investigating multidisciplinary effects of various treatments and moral choices of critical control variables across the multidisciplinary systems.

The S_j-systems and their inter-variable relations as a large sequence of endogenously interrelated functions can be log-linearized as in respect of expression (2.3). Yet in respect of the knowledge-induction of all the variables and coefficients by $\{(\theta(\varepsilon))\}$, the non-linearity of the log-linear form is submitted to evaluation of the relations in terms of dynamic learning coefficients. In the unified single system case, the endogenous variables evaluated by simulation method are selected in the standardized ratio forms like [(health variables)/(illness variables)] or stability form of [(health variables)/(economic variables)], [(health variables)/(illness variables)], etc. Around such ratio-variables the present days coronavirus debate is raging globally in respect of lockdown versus reopening the economy. In multiple interacting cases, both unified 'good' treatment cases as stated earlier can be the vector choices of 'good' variables. Or there can be a curative reformation of mutation cells into normalcy by the intensity of the episteme of unity of knowledge. Such a case is explained by Figure 2.1.

The wellbeing objective function shown previously can be deconstructed into many systems while maintaining the nature of complementarities between the variables as shown. Thereby, the intrinsic consciousness attribute $\{\epsilon\}$ of knowledge and the knowledge-induced variables spanning over knowledge, space, and time is also an endogenous variable in respect of its continuum effect on the increase or decrease of belief and commitment on the other endogenous variables and elements. In this regard there is this subtle quote on consciousness that we can invoke pertaining to the study of phenomenology of the entire Tawhidi ontological formalism (Kaku, 2015, p. 43, op. cit.): "Consciousness is the process of creating a model of the world using multiple feedback loops in various parameters (e.g. in temperatures, space, time, and in relation to others), in order to accomplish a goal (e.g. find mates, food, shelter)." Kaku calls this definition of phenomenological consciousness as the 'space-time theory of consciousness.' The microscopic power of consciousness in deepening of belief and its contrariness is quoted in the Qur'an (14:24–26).[11]

Conclusion: interactive, integrative, and evolutionary learning systems (IIE)

There is a subtle organically interrelated picture of unity of being and becoming by the interactive, integrative, and evolutionary learning processes in 'everything.' In this category of issues and problems there are the treatments of coronavirus away from its chaotic mutated state and towards a sustainable normalcy state. Our study in this chapter has proved that the model of Tawhidi ontological unity of knowledge is an analytical method of indicating and quantifying the direction of change in respect of the wellbeing criterion along with its semblance of sustainability in gaining normalcy. Such a model has proved to be a mathematical one. Unlike the trend of the coronavirus curve towards flattening, which is also a statistical indicator, the wellbeing function is a comprehensive measure of trend towards normalcy under the impact of unity of knowledge in terms of multidisciplinarity of diverse systems with the properties of interaction, integration, and evolutionary learning. We have shown this nature of the coronavirus normalcy curve in Chapter 1. In later chapters we will further amplify on the extensiveness of the ontological mathematical model of Tawhidi unity of knowledge by including issues of science, economy, society, institutions, and public policy with the overall moral inclusiveness for explaining the integral behavioural impact in gaining the normalcy picture in 'everything.'

Notes

1 Barrow, J.D. (1991). "Laws", in his *Theories of Everything, the Quest for Ulti-mate Explanation*, pp. 12–30, Oxford University Press, Oxford.
2 Gruber, T.R. (1993). "A translation approach to portable ontologies", *Knowl-edge Acquisition*, 5:2, pp. 199–200.
    Maxwell, G. (1962). "The ontological status of theoretical entities", in H. Feigl & G. Maxwell, eds. *Minnesota Studies in the Philosophy of Science, Vol. II: Sci-entific Explanation, Space and Time*, pp. 3–27, University of Minnesota Press, Minneapolis, MN.
3 Pickety, T., trans. & Goldhammer, A. (2017). *Capital in the Twenty-First Cen-tury*, Belknap Press of Harvard University Press, Boston, MA.
    Wallerstein, I. (1980). *The Modern World-System*, Academic Press, New York, NY.
4 Quinton, A. (1989). *Utilitarian Ethics*, Open Court, La Salle, IL.
5 Fischetti, M. & Krzywinski, M. (June 2020). *Scientific American*.
6 Imam Ibn Qayyim al-Jauziyah, trans. & Johnston, P. (1998). *Medicine of the Prophet*, Islamic Text Society, London, UK.
7 Qur'an (2:261). "And [recall] when you said, "O Moses, we can never endure one [kind of] food. So call upon your Lord to bring forth for us from the earth its green herbs and its cucumbers and its garlic and its lentils and its onions." [Moses] said, "Would you exchange what is better for what is less? Go into [any] settlement and indeed, you will have what you have asked." And they were covered with humiliation and poverty and returned with anger from Allah [upon them]. That was because they [repeatedly] disbelieved in the signs of Allah and killed the prophets without right. That was because they disobeyed and were [habitually] transgressing."
8 Choudhury, M.A. (2012). "On the existence of learning equilibriums", *Journal for Science*, 16:2, pp. 49–62.
9 Daly, H.E. (1992). "From empty-world to full-world economics: Recognizing an historical turning point in economic development", in R. Goodland, H.E. Daly, S. el-Serafy & B. von Droste, eds. *Environmentally Sustainable Economic Development: Building on Brundtland*, pp. 29–40, UNESCO, Paris, France.
10 WHO, "Programme Budget, 2012–2013" (PDF). WHO. Retrieved March 15, 2020.
11 Qur'an (14:24–26). "Have you not considered how Allah presents an exam-ple, [making] a good word like a good tree, whose root is firmly fixed and its branches [high] in the sky? It produces its fruit all the time, by permission of its Lord. And Allah presents examples for the people that perhaps they will be reminded. And the example of a bad word is like a bad tree, uprooted from the surface of the earth, not having any stability".

3 Wellbeing and sustainability

Lessons from coronavirus episode in the light of Tawhidi unity of knowledge

Introduction

We have pointed out in Chapter 2 that the operational nature of multidisciplinary unification based in unity of knowledge as of the moral and social inclusiveness of science, technology, and medicine is expressed by mathematical realism. The derived mathematical construction of the underlying worldview in the treatment and measurement of pandemic intensity positively or negatively in the curative scale is found to abide permanently in the primal ontological origin and continuum of monotheistic unity of knowledge. Its multidisciplinary existence (Being as Law) is found to pervade in and across 'everything.' In the present chapter our objective is to formalize such an abstracto-empirical nature of the imminent mathematical model based on the Tawhidi[1] methodology applied to the multidisciplinary approach to pandemic treatment and cure to normalcy. The same model also quantifies and analyzes the depth of the pandemic episode. It also determines the reversal of the pandemic episode to normalcy, thus formalizing the wellbeing objective criterion.

Conceptual inception of the mathematical construction of multidisciplinary pandemic methodology

We refer back to the primal organic embedding of being as law and its corporeal and conceptual representations in the act of becoming by way of unity of knowledge and so also by its contrariety. The following is the foundational representation of knowledge embedding in 'everything.' Its multidisciplinary systemic spreading and unification is of an overarching nature. Indeed, as we have explained in Chapter 1 the essential nature of the methodological and formal approach to treatment of pandemic mutative phenomena into normalcy can be explained by the following symbolism:

$\{\varepsilon_i\}$, i=1,2, . . . denotes the core ontological elements in terms of their knowledge induction that instils consciousness by a continuously unfolding of moral inclusiveness by unity of being and becoming in respect of 'everything' that is investigated. In the case of a pandemic treatment of all kinds these consciousness elements can denote a deeper sense of unity of moral inclusiveness in their investigated details and regarding the ensuing issues. Cleanliness is an attribute that expands and interactively integrates by cause and effect between cleanliness of the heart, soul, and practice in real world abidance. The principle of sharing and spreading out resources to the growing population of the poor, the deprived, the unemployed, the homeless, and the hungry invoke deepening consciousness of moral duty and practice. Such inner practices are applied to the consciousness of lockdown, social distancing and face masks, mutual social consultation. All these induce human resource training to uphold control and abide by the underlying conscious practices. Intensification of such morally inclusive consciousness gained by interaction and integration along with increasing evolutionary learning complements the elements of the total phenomenological aspect of unity of knowledge by the law of being and becoming in the order and scheme of 'everything.'

Formulating around $E(e) = \{e\}$

We thereby write in $E(..)$ functional form of inter-attribute circular causation relations:

$$e_j = E_k(\mathbf{e}_k); \ \mathbf{e} = (e_j, \mathbf{e}_k), \ i = (j, k) = 1, 2, \ldots \quad (3.1)$$

Bold symbols denote vectors. It is thereby noted that the attributes $\{e_i\}$ as sequence of consciousness (e.g. inner and outer moral-material cleanliness) are exogenously assigned by the ontological text of law (monotheistic unity of law as being). Yet the dynamics of complementarities between these attributes are explained by the inter-attribute of circular causation signified by their endogenous relations through the multivariates.

Particular cases

The ethics of consumption leads human habits away from eating carnivorous meat into their abandonment. This change in consumption habit in turn changes into further change towards purity and cleanliness by abandoning consumption of blood-clusters and blood-coagulated meat. Islamic ethics forbids eating ordinarily permissible things in which the name of Allah has not been invoked and cruelty in killing has been inflicted. Purity, humaneness, and cleanliness in increasing observance are intrinsic elements of consumption for good health as the environmental, individual, and social functions. Such attributes enter the control of pandemic situations by moral values of environmental, consumption, health purity, hygienic, and social abidance.

There are other very critical issues that can be addressed for resolution by the moral attribute embedding approach explained earlier. Consider the following cases while leaving out more for a later chapter: first, stemming the tide of unemployment in pandemic-like critical situation; and second, arresting the outburst of poverty and deprivation in pandemic-like critical situation.

The attribute composition of employment (unemployment) can be assigned to consciousness in job sharing at the widest institutional, social, and industrial levels. An approach of this type was recommended by the Organisation for Economic Co-operation and Development (OECD) during the high unemployment times of stagflation in the western world of the eighties. Job sharing in turn is a function of readiness towards restructuring wages to allow for job sharing and make the economic opportunities, income, and wage distributional considerations equitable and charitable for each other as an inculcated human value in science, society, and economy at large. Thereby, the methodological individualism by the scarcity notion of rational economic choice is replaced by the extensive *res extensa* and *res cogitans* principle of socio-economic complementarities (Descartes, 1954).[2]

Organic interrelations between conscious attributes in knowledge formation

The meaning, expression, and application of unity in organic inter-attribute relations like

$$e_j = E_k(\mathbf{e_k}); \mathbf{e} = (e_j, \mathbf{e_k}), i = (j, k) = 1, 2, \ldots \tag{3.2}$$

are thus borne to establish complementarities at large and annul the economic rationality choice of scarcity and marginal rate of substitution in mainstream economics (Holton, 1992).[3] The inter-attribute complementary linkages thus further extend to overarch into materiality as objects of moral and social sharing. In the Islamic value system of resource sharing such complementary artefacts of consciousness are invoked by the principle of zakat (Islamic charity) as a definite financial take on cashable wealth for ameliorating wellbeing of the deserving recipients, the absolute poor, the deprived, and the needy. In the conscious sense of attributes, collection and distribution of zakat ought to be organized in its moral (Islamic belief) and social sense (unity of being and becoming of monotheistic oneness) (Qur'an 73:20).[4] Such attributes with their extended implication at the level of moral-materiality combination marks the consciousness and willingness by the Qur'an ingrained in Tawhid as the singular monotheistic law.

In times of all kinds of pandemic that adversely affect wellbeing, as is the case of coronavirus episode, unemployment and deepening poverty were on the one side marked by lockdown that disabled livelihood. On the other side, there was the possibility of enabling economic and social activities. Yet the attribute approach to inner and outer complementary decision-making suggests orderly and organized balance of arrangement of pandemic control and enforced lockdown. Indeed, shared employment across friendly industries and economic diversification as in complementary rural-urban-service sectors production and employment maintenance is an effective way to control poverty in times of pandemic by means of avoiding the stoppage of labor force participation. The best sectoral selection that can be conceptualized and planned by the attributes of complementarities consciously is the life-fulfillment needs-economy against the wants-economy in times of pandemic episode and beyond (Levine, 1988).[5] Imam Fakhruddin Razi referred to such attributes of life-fulfillment design of society as Ubudiyyah, meaning worship (Noor, 1998).[6] Such consciousness of the attributes invokes a wellbeing focus. This in turn excites thinking in the direction of structural changes in the social economy at large (Choudhury ed. 2016).[7]

Reverse causality of attributes arising from the consciousness of the physical world-system

The previous discussion centering on inter-causality linkages has focused on (Attributes ⇔ Attributes) and with extension to (Attributes in consciousness ⇒ Moral-Materiality in consciousness ⇒ Sustainability of attributes in continuity of consciousness). Example in this regard is of the corona-economy that hit the world-system in the Great Depression of the 30s. It was then that bond financing of debt was pursued to get the economy out of depression and into recovery. This state of economic depression can be taken as the artefactual prevalence of interest-based bond financing. In the Islamic financing principle such a debt financing is disapproved on moral-material grounds of its inappropriateness. The conscious moral-materiality dawns, according to the Islamic worldview, by making cooperative ventures of the real economy and the sharing principle of the Islamic social economy as the moral and social structure of stability and sustainability of the economy and society. In the real economy the principle of continuous resource mobilization of savings into life-fulfillment joint venture types of investments results in sustained economic recovery. Keynes associated such a state of economic recovery with Savings=Investment as the way towards production of full-employment real output, and thereby attaining macroeconomic stability (Ventelou, 2005).[8] In the structure of Islamic economy the condition S=I remains a continuous phenomenon. Hence, real economic activity is continuously maintained in the absence of interest rate (riba). The life of the economy is permanently sustained with the real economy of productive rates of return replacing financial interest rates.

The conscious moral-material state of the productive economy is structured around the attribute of avoidance of interest rate by the real rate of return. This attribute is a key principle of the qur'anic law of Islamic economy and society. The design of the Islamic economy as moral-material attribute is thus consciously transmitted into advancement of the moral attribute extensively. The design of the economic and social system around avoidance of interest rate and the learning and willingness of individuals, institutions, communities, and societies extending outwards to the global extant of wellbeing is a moral and material attribute of deep import. It emanates from the inner comprehension and belief in moral-material attribute and instils into the practicality of the wider system of planned attributes causing these to actualize. Its wider implications are most fulfilling in the organic interrelations between the attributes of conscious belief and its moral-materiality structures. This is true vice versa via circular causation relations between the variables induced by knowledge instilled with consciousness as attributes.

The conscious actualization of interdependent attributes and their organic circular causation relations with the conscious attributes of moral-materiality and vice versa in organic circular causation make up the endogenous structure of organic being. Yet the attributes and their knowledge induction are exogenous elements of the primal ontological beginning of Tawhidi law of unity of knowledge. The logical formalism of the imminent structures of the consequential endogenous relations generate continuous moral, social, scientific, and economic expansion. Thereby, the conception of full employment attributed to Keynesian general macroeconomic equilibrium is annulled. It is replaced by the objective criteria of wellbeing and sustainability.

From the ontological domain of attributes to the epistemic formation of knowledge according to the Tawhidi law of unity of knowledge

Keeping in view the endogenously circular causation complementary relationship between consciousness attributes of the order of abstraction and instilled belief, knowledge is induced by such attribute properties.

Knowledge defined in the Tawhidi primal ontological law of universal complementarities between the good choices in contradiction to the unwanted choices (de-knowledge) is explained by the sequence of inter-causality of attributes that premise on functional ontologies as follows:

$$\theta = E(\varepsilon); \tag{3.3}$$

$$e_j = E_k(\mathbf{e}_k); \tag{3.4}$$

$$\mathbf{e} = (e_j, \mathbf{e}_k), \tag{3.5}$$

$$i = (j, k) = 1, 2, \ldots$$

The sequential notation for quantitative evaluation of knowledge is,

$$\{\theta\} = E(\{\varepsilon\}). \tag{3.6}$$

Thus, knowledge is the ontological emergence of functional relations of attributes in their various forms of conscious commitments. These functional interrelations are universally centered in the Tawhidi ontological law of unity of knowledge. We have explained this cardinal Islamic order of oneness regarding the world-system of 'everything' by the principle of organic unity of being and becoming.

It is to be noted that attributes are not quantitatively measured entities. They are simply instilled degrees and depths of consciousness to actualize. The result of such a vast domain of human consciousness results in the diversity of knowledge generation. Knowledge functionally emanating from organic interrelations of attributes also results in diverse verities. Yet all are centered on the primal ontological law of Tawhidi oneness. Thus, this cardinal law is the unique characteristic of both attributes and knowledge generation in the order of conscious commitment embedded in 'everything.' We write the immanence of attribute and knowledge generation based on the Tawhidi ontological premise in the following schema (Table 3.1):

Table 3.1 Immanence of attribute as foundational knowledge component in Tawhidi unity of knowledge

Tawhidi immanence of primal knowledge	Generating of practical knowledge as the episteme of unity of knowledge arising from the primal ontological premise $\{\theta\}$	An example in the case of moral-material complementarity in the light of the ontology of unity of knowledge and the epistemological mapping

Attributes → Primal knowledge

$E(\{\varepsilon\})$ → $\{\theta_P\}$

Exogenous consequences but endogenous organic attribute interrelations → endogenous consequence of attributes by organic interrelations

Emanation of Tawhid as law of primal ontology of knowledge in 'everything'

→ S=S(Ω) as the worldly monotheistic mapping of parts of Ω in the light of organic unity of knowledge as the primal ontology embodied in Ω as law. Thus, $S = S(\Omega) = S(\Omega(\mathbf{e}), E(\varepsilon))$ is well-defined and is well-defined continuously as parts of the revealed law $\Omega(\varepsilon)$ are explained via $\{\varepsilon\}$.

'S' (Islamic sunnah): sermons on the effectiveness of social distancing modes of Islamic regular prayers in mosques and otherwise. Thus in terms of attributes: consciousness in attributes ⇔ consciousness in moral-material attributes ⇔ attributes in continuity of consciousness) $E(\{\varepsilon\})$ ⇒ effectiveness of such advice. $\{\theta_p(\varepsilon) \in \Omega\}$.

$\{\theta_P(\varepsilon)\} = E(\{\varepsilon\})$ is the absolutely exogenous primal ontology of Tawhidi unity of knowledge. It is embedded in the nature, shape, form, order, and scheme of the generality and details of 'everything.' This part of knowledge generation commencing from attributes marks the seat of foundational consciousness to further comprehend the world-system under investigation. As the Tawhidi law of unity of knowledge,

$\Omega = [\{\theta_P(\mathbf{e})\} = E(\{\varepsilon\})$
⟶ $[\Omega,S]$ ⟶ $\{\theta\}$:

Exogenous ontological determinant with inner endogenous organic inter-attribute relations with each other and with $\{\theta_P(\varepsilon)\}$.

The epistemic generation of knowledge by discourse characterized by interaction, integration, and evolutionary learning intra- and inter-multidisciplinary systems for determining pervasive complementarities between choices for wellbeing in accordance with the ontological origin of Tawhidi unity of knowledge, while evading 'de-knowledge' as methodological individualism shown by pandemic mutations.

Formation of the world-system in the framework of Tawhidi unity of knowledge: from pandemic mutation to normalcy

The epistemological dynamics of deriving knowledge from the Tawhidi ontological law of unity of knowledge is foothold to practicality of its abstracto-empirical use. The result of such intra- and inter-system dynamics is denoted by the application of Tawhidi law of organic unity of knowledge by the repetitive use of simulacra (Fritzpatrick, 2003)[9] towards intensifying interaction leading to integration and then to evolutionary learning in knowledge, space, and time dimensions under the impact of knowledge-induction everywhere and in 'everything.' Thus, the universe sings the tune of Tawhidi ontological knowledge ingrained by its attributes.

As it was explained in Chapter 1 a systemic treatment for resolution into normalcy away from mutation is represented in spanning of the world-system in its following form: Let X_N denote a vector of normalcy variables. Let X_M denote a vector of mutation variables. Thereby, $(X_N/X_M)[\theta]$ denote the observable normalcy variables of various kinds relative to various mutation variables. With appropriate treatments denoted by say $T(\theta)$ with the organic interrelations like, $(\theta\uparrow\downarrow) \leftrightarrow (T(\theta))(\uparrow\downarrow) \leftrightarrow (X_N/X_M)(\theta)(\uparrow\downarrow)$, respectively by $(\uparrow\downarrow)$ as the case may be in respect of knowledge of normalcy $(\uparrow)$ or 'de-knowledge' of mutation $(\downarrow)$. In diagrammatic representation we show the circular causation relations as follows. Double directional arrows imply inter-variables endogenous circular causality when induced by knowledge $\{\theta\uparrow\}$ or 'de-knowledge' $\{\theta\downarrow\}$; and by the organic circular causation dynamics between the knowledge ('de-knowledge') epistemic variables and its induced world-system variables.

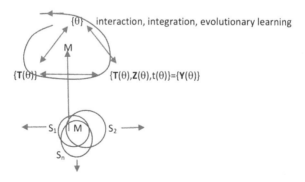

Figure 3.1 Configuring the complementary structure of multidisciplinarity in simulacra of evolutionary learning by unity of knowledge

The expanse of the entire relationship of the endogenous inter-variable circular causation occurs in knowledge, space, and time dimensions. This expression is denoted by $\{\theta,\{T(\theta),Z(\theta)\},t(\theta)\}$; with $\theta \in [\Omega(\varepsilon,\theta_p(\varepsilon)),$ $S(\theta_p(\varepsilon))]=$ plim$\{\theta\}$, with the properties of evolutionary learning in continuum. There is continuously the showering of wellbeing all the way commonly induced by knowledge in the multidisciplinary domain 'M.' Multidisciplinarity is explained by organically learning complementarities between intra- and inter-systems, S_i, $i = 1, 2, . . , n, ...$

Furthermore, the three-dimensional scale of the previous depiction is an evolutionary cross-sectional spectrum. This can be generalized to indefinitely n-dimensional expansionary spheroid as shown next. The domain 'M' is the organic interactive, integrative, and evolutionary learning (IIE) ground of multidisciplinarity defined by the Tawhidi principle of unity of knowledge across diversity of systems forming together the evolutionary learning world-system evaluated by simulacra of evolutionary wellbeing criteria in sustainability of the knowledge, space, and time continuum.

In the case of coronavirus pandemic the organic randomized control trials (RCTs) denoted by $\{T(\theta)\}$ affect all variables of the curative wellbeing function in stages of simulacra. Consequently, pandemic is cured progressively and sustained in curative continuum. The complementary inter-variable causality acts as the element of sustainability. The pandemic treatment effects remain curative over the long run. We have exemplified such a case in respect of the Prophet Muhammad's medicine that can be refined and innovated in progressive stages of RCTs. A worst kind of existing pandemic is poverty. In this condition, while survival is critical objective

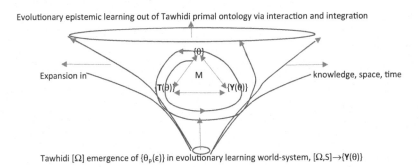

Evolutionary epistemic learning out of Tawhidi primal ontology via interaction and integration

Expansion in

knowledge, space, time

$\{\theta\}$

M

$\{T(\theta)\}$ $\{Y(\theta)\}$

Tawhidi $[\Omega]$ emergence of $\{\theta_p(\varepsilon)\}$ in evolutionary learning world-system, $[\Omega,S]\rightarrow\{Y(\theta)\}$

Figure 3.2 Conical display of evolutionary multidisciplinary ensemble across learning world-system

in wellbeing, the abject poverty-afflicted ones lose hope and desire to survive. They tend to love their terminal state in their despair of survival for tomorrow. Coronavirus and the like of pandemic do not matter for such terminally despairing ones. The universe has entered this fatal reality of poverty qua pandemic of which the present study of economics, society, and science has no coterminous answer, and no method out of RCTs (Banerjee & Duflo, 2012).[10] Indeed, poverty is a multifaceted state of human disempowerment (Sen, 1986).[11] Poverty alleviation requires a gamut of participatory instruments (UNDP, 1999).[12]

The figures shown earlier expatiate the complementary dynamics of unity of knowledge in the Tawhidi methodological worldview that adopt its socio-scientific methods to cause coexistence of cure by treatment and the instrumental variables in the scale of complementarity. This approach is contrary to marginalism denoting methodological individualism. Hence mutation is a social and physical form of relationship that is contrary to the extensive order of unity of being and becoming in unity of knowledge. The contrariety is ingrained in mainstream economics, and social, scientific, and technological ideas as physical and social Darwinism devoid of God (Dawkins, 2006).[13]

Modelling of wellbeing criterion in the world-system of pandemic treatment and cure

The emergence of the objective criterion that we refer to as wellbeing function is a sequential consequence from the beginning to the continuity of Tawhidi ontological application as explained by Figure 3.2. We define the wellbeing criterion as the unique objective of organizing the generality, particularities, and details of the world-system in terms of diverse problems and ensuing variables in the light of the pervasively complementary organic relations between these entities by the Tawhidi ontological principle of unity of knowledge. In search of the organic inter-causal relations between the knowledge-induced variables a large system of imminent equations of the endogenous variables is evaluated, that is by estimation followed by simulation of the coefficients. The emergent policy analysis and recommendations with further new simulated formulations of the wellbeing function with its entirety of inter-variable equations then follow.

The way to dispense the Prophet's medicine in its complementary form researched along with modern medicinal treatment as regular coronavirus pills is to take it regularly in daily intake with food. Besides this medicinal intake attributes like cleanliness and shared attributes of good behaviour, psychology, communitarian sociality, and faith are necessary ingredients of pandemic recovery. Other associated moral values are knowledge inculcation and human resource development towards communitarianism and participatory social contract for avoiding poverty, disease, and disorder. These practices ought to be carried out within the regular intake of the prophetic pills and guidance made and applied widely by extending their sources to the natural world of life-fulfilling plenty. Such prophetic guidance regarding protection from coronavirus can be assimilated with modern socio-scientific practices.[14]

Contrary examples to the complementary practices established wrongfully in sustainable adherence with wilful commitment are ignoring of civic duty to uphold norms of pandemic balanced lockdown, balanced industrial work habits, and orderliness of social distancing and face masks, wearing of proper and clean protective attire, eating of healthy food and diet, collectively establishing the social contract of participatory development of life-fulfillment economic activities, and importantly human empathy in the global and communitarian sense. It is also required to take such like adoptions in the consciousness of attributes of knowledge, and moral, social, and healthful choices with collaborative civic moral spirit. J. Graham (Mar. 21, 2020, 10:00 p.m. MDT)[15] writes, "The coronavirus crisis is a moral test. Will we pass? The challenges facing Americans are revealing our individual and national character." Indeed, society and the global whole are communities that learn by the evolutionary learning minuscule of self and family through the attribute properties of interaction, integration, sustained learning, and recursive practices of extensive complementarities (Vanek, 1971).[16]

Construction of quantitative form of wellbeing function from primal attributes to knowledge-induced empiricism: example from coronavirus episode

The derivation of knowledge from the Tawhidi ontological origin of unity of knowledge and signified by positive inter-variable complementarities is derived as an empirical objective criterion in respect of the wellbeing function. The cure of the coronavirus incidence by diversity of treatments on the inter-variable endogenous relations by way of complementarities is thereby established by empirical evaluation. First, evaluation comprises estimation of the large-scale system of equations in respect of their coefficients to bring out the degree of complementarities found between the variables. Second, estimation is then repeated by simulation of the coefficients under different conditions of inter-variable complementarities. Such evaluated complementarities signified by positive transformation of coefficients imply the degree of cure of the mutative state of coronavirus into normalcy state by inter-variable complementarities between the treatments.

The quantitative model of the wellbeing function is now formulated as follows:

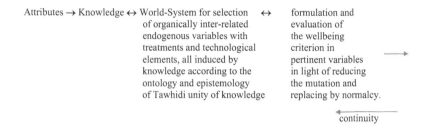

Figure 3.3 Continuous interaction, integration, and evolutionary learning in knowledge, space, and time dimensions of continuum

The wellbeing objective criterion function is now formulated as follows:

$$W(\theta(\varepsilon)) = W(\mathbf{Y}(\theta(\varepsilon))=\{\mathbf{Z}(\theta(\varepsilon)),\mathbf{T}(\theta(\varepsilon)), t(\theta(\varepsilon))\}, \qquad (3.7)$$
$$\text{where, } \mathbf{Y}(\theta(\varepsilon))=\{\mathbf{Z}(\theta(\varepsilon)),\mathbf{T}(\theta(\varepsilon)), t(\theta(\varepsilon))\},$$

with, $\mathbf{Z}(\theta(\varepsilon))$ as the vector of relative variables between $\{x_n\}$, $h = 1, 2, \ldots, n_1$ health-related normalcy variables, and $\{y_m\}$, $m = 1, 2, \ldots, n_1$ mutation related variables. Thus, the vector of relatives, $\{x_n/x_m\}[(\theta(\varepsilon))]$ denote the comparative dynamics towards attaining normalcy while reducing the incidence of mutation, as $\{\theta(\varepsilon)\}\uparrow$ with $\{\varepsilon\}\uparrow$, monotonically. Thereby the dynamics of consciousness are upheld. These include cleanliness; structural economic change to balance off coronavirus lockdown with resulting economic activity; conscious adoption of complementary medicine between natural sourced medicine and laboratory-generated medicine; and upholding social participation by the principle of unity of knowledge. These attributes are contrary to semblances of methodological individualism and the like in multidisciplinary disaggregation.

Participatory modes of socio-scientific activity altogether interrelate within themselves and with $\{x_n/y_m\}[(\theta(\varepsilon))]\uparrow$, with $\theta(\varepsilon)\uparrow$ monotonically as with $\{\varepsilon\}\uparrow$. The interrelating treatments vector is denoted by $\mathbf{T}(\theta(\varepsilon)) = \{t_j(\theta(\varepsilon))\}$, $j = 1, 2, \ldots, r$. The multidisciplinary nature of inter-variable and systemic endogenous interrelations is established by interaction, integration, and evolutionary learning as pointed out in Figures 3.1–3.3.

The target of the evaluation of the wellbeing function by transforming mutation of coronavirus into normalcy by unity of knowledge organizes the entire multidisciplinary system as a complementary unit in the following form:

$$W(\theta(\varepsilon)) = A(\theta(\varepsilon))*\Pi_{n1,r}(x_n/y_m)^{n1}*t_j^{r}][\theta(\varepsilon)], \qquad (3.8)$$

The $[(n_1 + r) + 1]$ number of equations of circular causation between the interrelating variables including the last one is the quantitative form of the wellbeing function in terms of the knowledge variable. That is, the wellbeing function exists in two forms. First, the W(.) expression is the theoretical form. This theoretical form conveys the meaning of the epistemological origin of the wellbeing function in terms of the properties of the primal Tawhidi ontology of unity of knowledge. Second, the evaluated form of the theoretical wellbeing function appears in the form of knowledge parameter as the endogenously related variable to all the evaluated $Y(\theta(\varepsilon))$-variables by their circular causation relations. Thus, all variables and their equations and both forms of the wellbeing function are commonly induced by $(\theta(\varepsilon))$.

The non-linear wellbeing function in its two forms and the inter-variable circular causation relations are given by the following expressions:

Let $(x_{ni})[\theta(\varepsilon)]$ denote variables of increasing incidence of normalcy shown by flattening curve (see Chapters 1 and 2). These thereby show deepening of unity of knowledge as representation of increasing normalcy.

Let $(x_{mi})[\theta(\varepsilon)]$ denote variables of decreasing incidence of mutation shown by the flattening curve. There is thereby a deepening of unity of knowledge as representation of dying of mutation and gaining on increasing normalcy.

Thus the complementary impact of all $\{x_{ni}/x_{m1}\}[\theta(\varepsilon)]$-ratio variables on wellbeing is ontologically derived by the precept of unity of knowledge into its practice in evaluating the effect of relative gains of treatment affecting normalcy relative to mutation. The underlying assumption here is that of evolutionary learning affecting progressive but not optimal resolution of normalcy contra mutation. Yet this is the continued achievement of stability and sustainability of a correcting healthful society under the impact of the principle of unity of knowledge affecting paired unity across systems of complementarities in socio-scientific engagement for attaining wellbeing.

Next we consider the effectiveness and sustainability of treatments $\{t_j(\theta(\varepsilon))\}$, $j = 1, 2, \ldots, r$ in establishing inter-variable resolution of normalcy relative to mutation of coronavirus states. Such effectiveness occurs progressively by complementarities along with the evolutionary learning impact of unity of knowledge.

The presence of the time-variable, $\{t(\theta(\varepsilon))\}$, induced by evolutionary learning along the path of stability and sustainability, marks the degrees of stability in sustainability. Thereby, the inter-causal path of effectiveness of the socio-scientific inter-variables and treatments is gained progressively along the vector trend of dynamic evolutionary learning path. Yet such is not an optimal path of the variables and their wellbeing objective criterion.

The economic, scientific, social, and moral representative variables exemplify the inter-variable mutuality by their complementarities in their absolute or relative forms. Thereby, sustainability of inter-variable relations by way of treatments over repeated applications to the wellbeing objective function appears by reproduction of unity of knowledge over time. The knowledge-induced wellbeing function conveying its patterns of impact on the multidisciplinary perspective of the new socio-scientific and reconstituted moral and behavioural social contract is the great lesson to learn from the science-economy-society model of moral inclusiveness concerning the problem of coronavirus episode as exemplar.

Complete wellbeing function

The entire evolutionary learning vector, $Y(\theta(\varepsilon))$, in knowledge, space, and time continuum, $\{\{Z(\theta(\varepsilon)), T(\theta(\varepsilon)), t(\theta(\varepsilon))\}$, in the multidisciplinary complementarities of inter-variable organic inter-causal relations is now represented by the following inter-relational system in dynamic log-linear form of the knowledge-induced coefficients:

$$\text{Evaluate } W(\theta(\varepsilon)) = W(Y(\theta(\varepsilon)) = \{Z(\theta(\varepsilon)), T(\theta(\varepsilon)), t(\theta(\varepsilon))\} \quad (3.9)$$

This is the theoretical form of the wellbeing function premised on its ontological construction in respect of the precept of unity of knowledge, which is represented in respect of pervasive complementarities between the inter-causal variables. The logarithmic form with dynamic knowledge-induced coefficients generated by simulations is represented by,

$$\text{Evaluate } W(\theta(\varepsilon)) = A(\theta(\varepsilon))*\Pi_{n1,r}(x_n/y_m)^a{}_{n1}*t_j{}^r][\theta(\varepsilon)], \quad (3.10)$$

with $\{a_{n1}, r\}$ as coefficients at a period of time when a certain state of inter-variable complementarities and sustainability gain evolutionary learning grounds from mutation to normalcy.

The circular causation equations of interdependent endogenous variables are:

$$(x_{ni}/y_{mi})[\theta(\varepsilon)] = f_i(\Pi_{j'i,r}(x_{nj}/y_{mj})^a{}_j*t_k{}^{rk})[\theta(\varepsilon)]. \quad (3.11)$$

$$t_k(\theta(\varepsilon)) = g_k(\Pi_{k'l,j}(x_j/y_j)^a{}_j*t_l{}^{rl})[\theta(\varepsilon)] \quad (3.12)$$

$f_i(.)$ and $g(.)$ are functional relations of the corresponding equations. These functions can take arbitrarily many forms corresponding to their derivations from the premise of unity of knowledge and responding to the properties of interaction, integration, and evolutionary learning (IIE) of the variables.

There are now all together $(i + k) = 2n (= m) + k(= K)$-number of equations in the systems (3.11) and (3.12). These equations provide the predictors of the evaluated (estimated and simulated by changes of coefficients) variables. The resulting evaluated variables are first estimated and then simulated by discursive changes of coefficients in the light of attaining better inter-variable complementarities. The simulated coefficients read out the need for corresponding changes in relatives of variables and treatments. The evaluated endogenous variables are applied to obtain the quantitatively evaluated form of the wellbeing function in expression (3.10).

Some such choices of the relative variables, treatments, and their simulated forms are as follows: $\{x_{ni}\}$ = intensity of cleanliness; public civic obedience of balance in lockdown and economic activity; intensifying public policy enactment of structural reformation into life-fulfillment patterns of socio-economic development; entrepreneurial development in clean production and activity lines. The questionnaire survey data for such variables are obtained by the respondents' outlook on poverty alleviation, changes in educational and human resource development towards participatory global and national perspectives, etc.

$\{y_{mi}\}$ denotes phasing out of mutation behaviours like methodological individualism in its widest context; devolving socio-economic development away from sheer growth-oriented entrepreneurial and industrial development as of the capitalist order (Pickety, op. cit.); controlling pollution-generating industrial expansion; and replacing the attitude of belligerence with the industry of peace, that is 'butter' versus 'guns' for global coexistence by amicable learning, etc.

$\{t_k\}$ denotes the vector of treatments that complement with the increasing value of the relative variable $\{x_{ni}/y_{mi}\}$, with $\{x_{ni}\}\uparrow$, $\{y_{mi}\}\downarrow$ comparatively. The treatments vector is complementary with the beneficial choices of variable-relatives and treatments. Examples in this case are of medicine, vaccine, anti-body, and plasma tests as short-term palliative combined with herbal medicine for long-term sustained cure (Commission on Global Governance, 1995; Inglott, 1990).[17] Treatment vector should include development of globally coordinated socio-scientific research and development programs for halting of pandemic episode and its cure at universally acceptable levels of prices, costs of production, and accessibility by the common public and wellbeing. Socio-scientific treatments are thus interactively integrated within the entire outlook of science-economy-society moral inclusiveness.

All the time and in 'everything' the diversity of such interaction and integration between all vectors within $\{Y(\theta(\varepsilon)) = \{Z(\theta(\varepsilon)), T(\theta(\varepsilon)), t(\theta(\varepsilon))\}$ are based on evolutionary learning. The driving force of positive realization in all these domains is the ontology of unity of knowledge and the sustained actualization of consciousness in rounds of learning processes in unity of knowledge. The rise and sustainability of consciousness is carried through by the induction of attributes of knowledge in the generality and particulars of the socio-scientific world-system with the objective target of attaining

Table 3.2 Towards constructing the pandemic curative model according to Tawhidi unity of knowledge

Primal Ontology	Epistemology	Worldly Knowledge	World-System	Evaluation	Continuity
Of Tawhidi Unity Of knowledge (monotheistic Oneness as law) Symbolism: Ω	as derivation of knowledge from Ω in its most generalized implication 'S'	in respect of the ontological-epistemic derivation of events in historical completeness $\{\theta\}$	spanned by knowledge, knowledge-induced space and knowledge-induced time: Spanning of Histories by Events: $\{E(\theta) = \{E\{\theta, X(\theta), t(\theta)\}$	of the world-system by simulation of the wellbeing function Evaluate $W(\theta)=W(\theta, X(\theta), t(\theta))$ subject to the properties of interaction, Integration,	of 'evaluation' in respect of derived inferences and possibility of simulacra of $W(\theta)$. Phenomenology
$[\Omega \supset S(\Omega) \supset \{\theta\}]$	$\rightarrow_f \{E(\theta)\}$	$\rightarrow_w$ Eval.$_{,\{E(\theta)\}}$ $\{W(\theta)\}$ Subject to Circular causation Relations in $\{\theta, X(\theta), t(\theta)\}$	$\rightarrow$Continuity	Evolutionary learning (Figures. 3.1 & 3.2): $X_i(\theta) \subset \{E_i,(\theta)\}$ $=\{f_i(E_j(\theta))\}$, $i, j = 1, 2, .. \ i \neq j$ $R\{\theta\} \subset \{F(E(\theta)\}$ $\Rightarrow \theta = F(E(\theta))$. Estimation is followed by simulation in 'evaluation.'	

Phenomenological recursive endogenous relations (RCTs)

Repeated endogenous RCT[18] circular causation relations in Tawhidi knowledge-induced string relation (TSR)

wellbeing. These attributes are shown in Table 3.2. It is noted that socio-scientific consciousness based on unity of knowledge induced by attributes marks overarching complementarities between moral assertions, materiality, and practical applications. The Qur'an asserts such organic soul-mind-body conscious interrelations in establishing a life-fulfilling society. Monotheistic faith has been unified with conscious attributes of behaviour and materiality.[19] Our specific case here is the study of socio-scientific dynamics of monotheistic unity of knowledge to turn pandemic mutative scenario into normalcy.

The focus of any and all varieties of socio-scientific studies in the light of the methodology of unity of knowledge is in respect of the following string chain that studies 'everything' in the continuum of knowledge, space, and time dimensions:

Interpreting the theoretical construction of the wellbeing function in coronavirus episode

There are no available data on the relationship between treatments and either confirmed cases or cured patients of coronavirus disease. Therefore, a complete statistical evaluation of the wellbeing function is only theoretically possible but yet instructive. World data (Our World in Data;[20] European CDC)[21] on comparative cumulative 'testing' and confirmation of incidence of coronavirus incidence shows that between December 2019 and June 2020, there existed conformable increases in cumulative number per million people (x_1) and in the rates of increase (x_2) in both of these indicators. Some statistical implications can be derived in this respect.

Consider the functional relationship of effectual wellbeing, $W(x_1/T,x_2/T)$, meaning the consequential effect of treatments 'T' on reduction of x_1 and x_2. Thereby, with the effectiveness of knowledge as unity between the variables x_1 and x_2 in respect of the 'T'-effect, the variables all together are under the influence of unity of knowledge signified by 'θ' affecting 'T' and thereby expectedly reducing $(x_1/T,x_2/T)[\theta]$.

$$
\begin{aligned}
dW(\theta)/d\theta &= [\partial W(\theta)/\partial(x_1/T)(\theta)]*[d(x_1/T)(\theta)/d\theta] \\
&\quad + [\partial W(\theta)/\partial(x_2/T)(\theta)]*[d(x_2/T)(\theta)/d\theta] \quad\quad (3.13) \\
&= T1*[d(x_1/T)(\theta)/d\theta] + T2*\ d(x_2/T)(\theta)/d\theta] \\
&= T1*[(1/T).(dx_1/d\theta) - (x_1/T^2)(dT/d\theta)] + T2*[(1/T). \\
&\quad (dx_2/d\theta) - (x_2/T^2)(dT/d\theta)] \\
&= [T1*[(1/T).(dx_1/d\theta) + T2*(1/T).(dx_2/d\theta)] - \\
&\quad (1/T)[(x_1/T)(dT/d\theta) + (x_2/T)(dT/d\theta)] > 0 \\
&= T*[T1*[(1/T).(dx_1/d\theta) + T2*(1/T).(dx_2/d\theta)] > \\
&\quad [(x_1/T)(dT/d\theta) + (x_2/T)(dT/d\theta)] > 0 \quad\quad (3.14)
\end{aligned}
$$

This result implies that there ought to be simultaneous compounded impact of complementary medicine, economy, society, and moral-material treatment of self, behaviour, and environment to realize the increase in wellbeing for pandemic cure. Such complementarities between medicinal and behavioural effectiveness are realized by the impact of $\{\theta\}$ as endogenous learning in unity of knowledge affecting the wellbeing criterion function and its circular causation relations. Yet data point out that treatment underlying increased cumulative testing does not reduce the increase and rate of increase in confirmed coronavirus cases. Thereby, the compounded applications and treatments in the context of their medical, economic, social, and moral inclusiveness remain ineffective. According to the discussion given earlier this result of coronavirus cure in the absence or weakness of inter-causal medical applications and complementarities between treatments is a cause of ineffective alleviation of coronavirus pandemic. Furthermore, expression (3.14) points to the complementary practice of medicine and treatment with the continuity of evolutionary learning by $\{\theta\}$ as a most desired area of implementation.

Conclusion

This chapter has provided the generalized model for studying the causes, effects, and controls of all kinds of pandemic consequences. Included in this broadest range of study are systemic treatments of multidisciplinary system-oriented interaction, integration, and evolutionary (IIE) learning in sustainability across a continuum of knowledge, space, and time dimensions. The centrepiece of this broadest spectrum of analytical study is the ontological theme of unity of knowledge signified by complementarities between the good choices of life. An example of such vectors of multivariate complementarities determined by their organic interrelations convey the inclusiveness of material aspects of health, life, treatments, and ethical abidance in behavioural, moral, social, and psychological practices of life.

All these factors of goodly and sustained treatments for the control of COVID-19 pandemic leading to the complementary way of realizing sustained results of randomized control trials can be explained by the following dynamics. Figure 3.4 here shows IIE learning in the complex multivariate and multidisciplinary prism resulting in outcomes of treatments of different types that together complement and interrelate in the wellbeing objective criterion.

The generalized multivariate form of the Input/Output (I/O) factors with organically unified (complemented) multivariate consequential vectors of multi-outcomes of randomized control trials (RCTs) of the wellbeing objective function is formalized as follows. The inherent nature of this formal model is not different from that explained in respect of expressions (3.7–3.12). Thus, the generalized methodological formalism and application of

Evolutionary Learning Systems of outputs (O's, x's, ()'s)
With continuous complex relations between nodes forming an
Inter-causally related spheroid (not fully drawn).

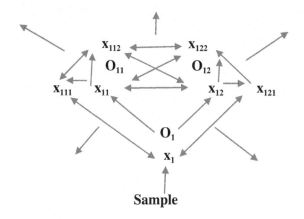

Sample

Figure 3.4 Randomized control trials (RCTs): multiple treatments by inter-causally
related systems (outcomes)

the wellbeing function with its organic unity of relations in terms of the
large system of endogenous circular causation relations between the variables is established.

Treatments (variables) → Outcomes:

$$\{x_j, x_{jk}, x_{jkl}, \ldots\}[\theta] \rightarrow \{O_i, O_{jk}, O_{jkl} \ldots\}[\theta] \qquad (3.15)$$
$$\Rightarrow \text{Compound functions, } O_i \cdot O_{jk} \cdot O_{jkl} \cdot \ldots = F(x_j, x_{jk}, x_{jkl}, \ldots)[\theta] \qquad (3.16)$$

The partial intra-system views of this generalized system of outcomes
resulting from randomized vectors of treatments are given by, $O_i = f_i(x_j(\theta))$,

$$O_{jk} = f(x_j, x_{jk})[\theta], \text{ etc.} \qquad (3.17)$$

Notes

1 Tawhid is the qur'anic term for monotheistic Oneness of Allah. As the universal
and unique law embodying 'everything' Tawhid can be explained by recourse to
the Qur'an in respect of the universal phenomena of organic unity of being and
becoming in the order and scheme of 'everything' (Qur'an 36:36). This extended

meaning of Tawhid as phenomenological explanation is given in *Towards Understanding the Qur'an* (Islamicstudies.info, Islamic Foundations UK) in the following words: "This is still another argument for Tauhid. Here again certain realities of daily experience have been mentioned and it is suggested that man observes these day and night but does not ponder over them seriously, whereas they contain signs and pointers to the reality. The coming together of the man and woman is the cause of man's own birth. Procreation among the animals also is due to the combination between the male and the female. Also about vegetation, man knows that the law of sex is working in it. Even among the lifeless substances when different things combine with one another, a variety of compounds come into existence. The basic composition of matter itself has become possible due to the close affinity between the positive and the negative electric charges. This law of the pairs which is the basis of the existence of the entire universe, contains in itself such complexities and fineness of wisdom and workmanship, and there exist such harmonies and mutual relationships between the members of each pair that an objective observer can neither regard it as the result of an accident, nor can he believe that many different gods might have created these countless pairs and matched their members, one with the other, with such great wisdom. The members of each pair being a perfect match for each other and coming into being of new things with their combination itself is an explicit argument of the Creator's being One and only One."

2 Descartes, R. (1954). "Discourse on method", in S. Commins & Linscott, R.N., eds. *Man & the Universe: The Philosophers of Science*, pp. 163–220, Pocket Books, Inc., New York, NY.

3 Holton, R.L. (1992). *Economy and Society*, Routledge, London.

4 Qur'an (73:20): ". . . . and establish regular prayers and give regular charity; and loan to Allah a beautiful loan. And whatever good ye send forth for your souls, ye shall find it in Allah's presence, Yea, better and greater in reward and seek ye the grace of Allah: for Allah is oft-forgiving, Most Merciful."

5 Levine, D. (1988). *Needs, Rights and the Markets*, Lynne Rienner Publishers, Boulder, CO.

6 Noor, H.M. (1998). "Razi's human needs theory and its relevance to ethics and economics", *Humanomics*, 14:1, pp. 59–96.

7 Choudhury, M.A. (2016). *God-Conscious Organization and the Islamic Social Economy*. Routledge, London.

8 Ventelou, B. (2005). "Economic thought on the eve of the general theory", in *Millennial Keynes*, Chapter 2, M.E. Sharpe, Armonk, NY.

9 Fitzpatrick, T. (2003). "Postmodernism and new directions", in P. Alcock, A. Erskine & M. May, eds. *Social Policy*, pp. 125–133, Blackwell, Oxford.

10 Banerjee, A. & Duflo, E. (20012). *Poor Economics, A Radical Rethinking of the Way to Fight Global Poverty*, Penguin.

11 Sen, A. (1986). "Exchange entitlement", in his *Poverty and Famines, an Essay on Entitlement and Deprivation*, pp. 167–173, Clarendon Press, Oxford.

12 UNDP (1999, p. 75): "Participation in the process must be widened. Knowledge is needed not only of the latest technologies but also of local ecosystems and food chains, local culture and systems of exchange, socio-economic conditions and political and market stability. This calls for broad collaboration."

13 Dawkins, R. (2006). *The Selfish Gene*, Oxford University Press, Oxford.

14 Prophet Muhammad advised: "Make use of medical treatment, for Allah has not made a disease without appointing a remedy for it, with the exception of one disease: old age."

Some other prophetic guidance during times of pandemic episodes are: (1) "Whoever wakes up from their sleep should wash their hands before putting them in the water for ablution, because nobody knows where their hands have been, during sleep." (2) "If you hear of an outbreak of plague in a land, do not enter it; but if the plague breaks out in a place while you are in it, do not leave that place." (3) "One who's sick should not be put with one who's healthy." (4) "Cleanliness is half of faith."

A Muslim is also permitted to temporarily suspend performing Islamic duties that might compromise their health, like, fasting, praying, or any others.

Taking care of individual and societal health, while integral, is only a small part of a perfect system that covers every aspect of life including politics, finance, family and relationship, work and education etc., all stitched in harmony to ensure that happiness that the Creator intended through his final message to all humans.

Source: www.guidetoislam.com

15 Graham, J. (Mar. 21, 2020, 10:00 pm MDT). "The coronavirus crisis is a moral test: Will we pass? The challenges facing Americans are revealing our individual and national character", *Deseret News*.
16 Vanek, J. (1971). "The participatory economy in a theory of social evolution", in his *The Participatory Economy: An Evolutionary and a Strategy for Development*, pp. 51–89, Cornell University Press, Ithaca, NY.
17 Inglott, P.S. (1990). "The rights of future generations: Some socio-philosophical considerations", in S. Busuttil, E. Agius, P.S. Inglott & T. Macelli, eds. *Our Responsibilities Towards Future Generations*, pp. 17–27, Foundation for International Studies & UNESCO, Malta.
   Commission on Global Governance (1995). "Global civic ethic", in *Our Global Neighbourhood, a Report of the Commission on Global Governance*, Oxford University Press, New York.
18 Randomized control trials (RCT) in Banerjee, A. & Duflo, E. (op. cit.).
19 Qur'an (7:85): "And to Madyan (We sent) their brother Shu'aib. He said: O my people! Serve Allah, you have no god other than Him; clear proof indeed has come to you from your Lord, therefore give full measure and weight and do not diminish to men their things, and do not make mischief in the land after its reform; this is better for you if you are believers."
20 https://ourworldindata.org/
21 www.bing.com/news/search?q=european+cdc&qpvt=european+cdc&FORM=EWRE

4 Normalizing pandemic episode by science-economy-society moral inclusiveness

Introduction

The central explanatory formalism of all pandemic, and thereby, of multidimensional factors of complementary relations in evaluating the objective criterion of wellbeing is the ontologically derived model of unity of knowledge between the good things of life by their organic endogenous circular-causation relations. The underlying model of this ontological derivation resulting in epistemic and followed by phenomenological implications, all together repeating in circular causation inter-variable relations, is explained. In this chapter the extension of the underlying formalism is studied in terms of a wider field of evaluation of the wellbeing criterion premised on its ontological groundwork. The emergent empirical work in this chapter thereby implies that the multivariate and multidimensional unity of knowledge is analytically studied in a vastly formal context.

The inherent interdependent variables and their relations appear in complex non-linear forms to combat the pandemic severity of many converging malaise that have been ignored in the combination of science, economic, social, and ethical treatments. The formulation of the wellbeing function for the treatment of coronavirus into a normalcy state necessitates a comprehensive approach that combines these diverse factors within their moral inclusiveness as an endogenously integrated comprehensive whole. We refer to this facet of the model as pervasively complemented multidisciplinary ensemble or the socio-scientific world-system arising from the ontology of unity of knowledge. In the qur'anic context this ontological primacy is called Tawhid. We treat Tawhid as the law of unity of knowledge between the good choices and those that can be converted from the avoidable categories into acceptable choices by relativity of their variable-relatives. All these feed into the wellbeing objective function and form inter-variable circular causation relations.

In the multivariate causes of pandemic consequences both incidence and cure suggest that large systems of complex and non-linear relations of mathematical computerized nature must be studied. The resulting logical formalism would span across the domains of ontology, episteme, and phenomenology continuously interrelating altogether to establish sustainability of the socio-scientific universe (world-system). The model of moral inclusiveness along with its various socio-scientific elements described by variables thereby comprise the resulting algorithmic model of science-economy-society moral inclusiveness. The epistemic features of the resulting multidisciplinary model of unity of knowledge developed for treatment of the pandemic case are shown in Figure 4.1.

Summarizing the Wellbeing Objective Criterion according to the episteme of unity of knowledge

Faith & Law	Simultaneity	Multidisciplinary	Functional evaluative	Properties of
Ontology/ Episteme	of knowledge and faith and	world-system unity of knowledge	ontology of being & becoming	continued (continua)
(unity of	otherwise	dissociative knowledge	(unity & mutation)	interaction,
Knowledge)		mutation	Wellbeing & otherwise	integration, evolutionary learning res extensa and
$\{\varepsilon\} \to _{(\Omega,S)}$	$\{\theta(\varepsilon)\} \to _{(\Omega,S)}$	$\{X(\{\theta(\varepsilon)\})\} \to_{W(\theta)}$	Evaluate $W(\{X(\{\theta(\varepsilon)\})\}$, subject to, inter-causality	res cogitans
			between variables in	$\to$ SUSTAINABILITY
			$\{X(\{\theta(\varepsilon)\})\}$ may be vectors	(continuity of
			of absolute value of vectors	evolutionary
			multidisciplinarity The choice of such variables	learning circular processes)
			can be by relatives of (good/bad). Example of such a unity of knowledge or Relative is (flattening or flattened coronavirus curve)/(peak otherwise: Evaluation Or nearing peak coronavirus curve) with sustainability and(estimation and simulacra) Wellbeing value as this relative vector declined by invoking the good things of life.	

$\{\theta(\varepsilon)\}\uparrow$ as $\varepsilon\uparrow$ and $\{\theta(\varepsilon)\}\downarrow$ as $\varepsilon\downarrow$.

Figure 4.1 Continuity of methodology of unity of knowledge by primal ontology of truth over the domain of continuum of knowledge, space, and time

Multidisciplinary unity of knowledge in large model formalism of pandemic-like consequences

Figure 4.2 exemplifies the previously mentioned model features in reference to the simplified three systems, S_1, S_2, S_3, with strongly inclusive multidisciplinary (Nicolau, 1995)[1] and multidimensional features. These features are explained by the properties of interaction, integration, and evolutionary learning (IIE). They exist as internally consistent with ontological, epistemological, phenomenological, and sustainable properties of regenerating pervasive and continuous intra- and inter-systemic organic interdependency. The generalized model of multidisciplinary unity of knowledge with such complementarities is the essential nature of science, society, and economic moral inclusiveness. The resulting large-scale model of unity of knowledge referred to here as the Wellbeing Function (criterion) is the universal and unique objective goal of pandemic treatment. It is based on the sustainability property across the continuum of the imminent learning model intra- and inter-systems. This idea of analytical continuum premised on the methodology of unity of knowledge conveys the meaning of organic complementarities between endogenous variables in all systems. A further important feature of the multidisciplinary intra- and inter-systemic model in Figure 4.2 is that both the integrated core (mathematical intersection of indefinitely many S's) and the periphery of the S's expand simultaneously, as indicated by the outward arrows. The impact of knowledge in such an evolutionary learning dynamic results in the density of the sets to yield the probability limiting points ($\text{plim}_{\{q\}}$) of the integrated core.

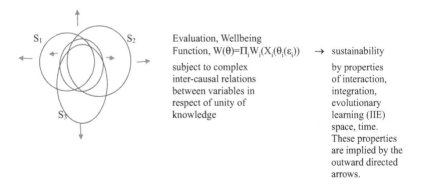

S_1 S_2 S_3

Evaluation, Wellbeing Function, $W(\theta) = \Pi_i W_i(X_i(\theta_i(\varepsilon_i)))$ → sustainability

subject to complex inter-causal relations between variables in respect of unity of knowledge

by properties of interaction, integration, evolutionary learning (IIE) space, time. These properties are implied by the outward directed arrows.

Figure 4.2 Concept of multidisciplinarity explained by the inter-systemic endogenously related vector of variables in the wellbeing function, $W\{X(\{\theta(\varepsilon)\})\}$

The wellbeing function is evaluated in respect of the inter-variable endogenously circular causation relations. Some of the multivariate cases of pandemic and unified multidisciplinary learning are mentioned next.

COVID-19 has been followed by rethinking on the scope of multidisciplinary ensemble; in the widening of social understanding beyond the sheer classical limitations (Lan, 2020)[2] in the fields of security of health, protection of the environment of all animate and inanimate entities, economy, and moral and social inclusiveness by great changes in psychological, behavioural, institutional, and socio-scientific conducts. Within this spanning gamut of new outlook in the global policy-theoretic considerations the nature of economic, social/ethical, and institutional perspectives of future organization of a holistic multidisciplinary ensemble emerges. The traditional nature of policies and institutional mind are changing (Bergoc & Andolsek, 2019).[3] The multivariate vector and consequential objective and its formalism are changing based on an altered methodological worldview of the underlying episteme. The meaning of episteme is conveyed by the multidisciplinary and holistic conception of experience that embraces the widening field of variables, choices, the objective goal, and abstraction along with empirical application.

On this methodological viewpoint of episteme Foucault wrote (quoted in Dreyfus & Rabinow, 1983, p. 18):[4]

> By episteme, we mean . . . the total set of relations that unite, at a given period, the discursive practices that give rise to epistemological figures, science, and possibly formalized systems. . . . The episteme is not a form of knowledge (*connaissance*) or type of rationality which, crossing the boundaries of the most varied sciences, manifests the sovereign unity of a subject, a spirit, or a period: it is the totality of relations that can be discovered, for a given period, between the sciences when one analyses them at the level of discursive regularities.

The multivariate pandemic treatment vector including monetary and fiscal effects

An example of the multivariate vector that specifically can be studied in terms of the mutual impact with monetary and fiscal policies, choices, and preferences is given next. Some plausible interrelations between the multivariate vector and monetary and fiscal policies in science-economy-society-wide planning that predominates in the pandemic case are as follows:

1 Ethics of consumption and food are complementary with monetary and fiscal expansion as policy responses either from the government side or

the market economy where morally inclusive preferences of consumption choices are made (Veblen, [1899] 1912),[5] (X_1).

2   Participatory socio-economic development in life-fulfilling needs are complementary to healthy choices of food and consumption in life-sustaining sectoral transformation wherein monetary and fiscal expansion contributes to the consequential advancement of the life-fulfillment socio-economic restructuring (Inglott, 1990),[6] (X_2).

3   Participatory sectors of socio-economic development by wellbeing instruments, for instance by replacing interest rate by real-economy indicators (X_3), enable advancement of the life-fulfillment regime of socio-economic development and all that such a transformation contributes to scientific, economic, and social moral inclusiveness in a holistic knowledge-induced multidimensional actualization.[7]

4   Needs against wants in real-economy development forms the hallmark of life-fulfilling socio-economic model of participatory development (Levine, 1988), (X_4).[8]

5   Healthy living as part of wellbeing with life-sustaining essentials of socio-economic development (Hawley, 1986),[9] (X_5).

6   Multidisciplinary educational reconstruction with a new paradigm of wellbeing and life-sustaining essentials while critically examining mainstream understanding of economy and society: human resource development and poverty alleviation essentiality (Holton, 1992),[10] (X_6).

7   Global forums for understanding and applying the multidisciplinary paradigm of participatory development, interaction, integration, and evolutionary learning among all establish the concerted global community in these respects, (X_7).

8   Output, income, and empowerment complement with life-fulfilling socio-economic development with wellbeing effects of poverty alleviation, human resource development, and enterprise (Streeten, 2014),[11] (X_8).

The inter-relational vector ($\mathbf{Z}(\theta)$) including monetary ($M(\theta)$) and fiscal ($F(\theta)$) variables is $\mathbf{Z}(\theta) = (M,F,X_1,X_2, \ldots,X_7)[\theta]$. Any positive monotonic transformation of this vector, say $f(\mathbf{Z}(\theta))$, is a complex interrelational vector of the $\mathbf{Z}(\theta)$-kind. The corresponding interrelated monetary and fiscal policy variables between them is dM/dF. The complementarity or substitution between monetary and fiscal policies in respect of the income/output variable ($Y(\theta)=X_8$) is implied by dM/dY, positive or negative, respectively. Likewise, for fiscal policy in relation to $Y(\theta)$-variable we have dF/dY, positive or negative, respectively. Various combinations of positive and negative values of dM/dY along with dF/dY, and thereby of dM/dF, can be appropriately interpreted with the other variables of the $\mathbf{Z}(\theta)$-vector.

In reference to the evolutionary learning parameter 'θ' of unity of knowledge implying holism of the multidimensional aspects of pandemic treatment and cure, all of the variables of $\mathbf{Z}(\theta)$-vector are induced by 'θ.' Figure 4.1 is now adopted to this phenomenon to first yield the wellbeing function, $W(\mathbf{Z}(\theta))$, for its evaluation (estimation and simulation) in respect of the circular causation relations between the $\mathbf{Z}(\theta)$-variables and the quantification of the knowledge parameter as linear approximation of the wellbeing function.

Selection of variables in the wellbeing function with monetary and fiscal effects of moral inclusiveness

The wellbeing objective criterion, $W(\mathbf{Z}(\theta))$, endogenizes interaction, integration, and evolutionary (IIE) learning in continuum of inter-variable relationship,[12] epistemically premised in unity of knowledge. The endogenous interrelations between the variables in the form of multidimensional elements of the pandemic world-system across the diversity of effects in knowledge, space, and time are explained by the circular causation equations of evaluating the wellbeing objective criterion. The formal expression of the wellbeing function along with its circular causation endogenous interrelations between the variables is given as follows:

$$\text{Evaluate}_{\{\theta\}} \, W(\mathbf{Z}(\theta)), \tag{4.1}$$

subject to the endogenous inter-variable circular causation (C.C.) relations of $\mathbf{Z}(\theta)$-vector,

$$x_i(\theta) = f_i(\mathbf{x}_j(\theta)), \, i, j = 1, 2, \ldots, 10 \text{ including M, F; } i \neq j \text{ as}$$
mentioned earlier are the C.C. equations $\tag{4.2}$

The last additional equation that quantitatively evaluates the wellbeing function in terms of the variables of $\mathbf{Z}(\theta)$ is,

$$\theta = W(\mathbf{Z}^{\wedge}(\theta)), \text{ where the hatted variables are the statistically}$$
evaluated $\mathbf{Z}(\theta)$-variables of the circular causation relations. $\tag{4.3}$

We now explain the specific circular causation relations in terms of M and F and all the other variables:

$$M(\theta) = f_1(F, \mathbf{x})[\theta], \text{ where } \mathbf{x}(\theta) = \{x_1, x_2, \ldots, x_8\}[\theta] \tag{4.4}$$

$$F(\theta) = f_2(M, \mathbf{x})[\theta], \text{ where } \mathbf{x}(\theta) = \{x_1, x_2, \ldots, x_8\}[\theta] \tag{4.5}$$

$$x_i(\theta) = f_i(M, F, \mathbf{x}_j)[\theta], \, i \neq j, \, (i, j) = 1, 2, \ldots, 8 \tag{4.6}$$

By taking all the previous equations in the log-linear form we can derive partial elasticity of F to M as $\in_{F,M}$. Likewise, the individual $x_i(\theta)$-partial elasticity of M is denoted by $\in_{xi,M}$; partial elasticity coefficients of F to x_i are denoted by $\in_{F,xi}$; partial elasticity coefficient of M to F is $\in_{M,F}$ ($\neq\in_{F,M}$); individual $x_i(\theta)$-partial elasticity to F is denoted by $\in_{xi,F}$; individual inter-$x_i(\theta)$-partial elasticity coefficient is $\in_{xi,xj}$, ($\neq\in_{xj,xi}$) (i, j) = 1, 2,. . .,8. These partial elasticity coefficients are quantified by the respective estimated and simulated (evaluated) partial coefficients of the logarithmic forms of the equations (4.2)-(4.6).[13] The partial elasticity coefficients are functions of 'θ.' They are therefore estimable followed by simulation – evaluative.

To find the monetary and fiscal impacts on the other variables and vice versa we proceed as follows: from equation (4.4) we derive first the percentage monetary policy impact,

$$\text{dlnM/dln}\theta = (\partial\ln f_1/\partial\ln F)*(\text{dlnF/dln}\theta)$$
$$+ \Sigma_{i=1}^{8}(\partial\ln f_1/\partial\ln x_i)*(\text{dlnx}_i/\text{dlnq}). \qquad (4.7)$$

The positive signs of $(\partial\ln f_1/\partial\ln F)$ and each of $(\partial\ln f_1/\partial\ln x_i)$ in the light of the focus of monetary and fiscal expansion on socio-economic development, the complementarity property of the variables of the wellbeing function of expression (4.1) with its circular causation equations yields dlnM/dlnθ > 0. This is a sustained result as long as the evolutionary learning proceeds on along the path of the corresponding complementarities. Thereby, the multidimensional treatments and curative attention must be sustained in respect of scientific, economic, societal moral inclusiveness.

By a similar implication of income multiplier effect and credit creation effect of monetary theory (Mankiw, 2016),[14]

$$\text{dlnM/dlnY} = (\partial\ln f_1/\partial\ln F)*(\text{dlnF/dlnY}) + \Sigma_{i=1}^{8}$$
$$(\partial\ln f_1/\partial\ln x_i)*(\text{dlnx}_i/\text{dlnY}) > 0. \qquad (4.8)$$

This result theoretically implies $(\partial\ln f_1/\partial\ln F)*(\text{dlnF/dlnY}) > 0$ by the complementary relationship between monetary, fiscal, and output. Likewise, each of $\partial\ln f_1/\partial\ln x_i > 0$ under the income multiplier effect on every complementary inputs of scientific, economic, and societal moral inclusiveness in socio-economic development.

A similar deductive result can be derived in respect of fiscal effects of the type given by monetary policy impact of complementary monetary policy and evolutionary learning and income effects on the various inputs of scientific, economic, and societal moral inclusiveness of socio-economic development.

Expression (4.7) implies that, in as far as M and F complement in the advancement and sustainability by knowledge induction of the life-ful-fillment regime of socio-economic development, so also the underlying scientific, economic, and societal moral inclusiveness sustain themselves (Stanford Encyclopedia of Philosophy, 2016).[15] Indeed, evaluation of the wellbeing objective criterion is constructed and sustained by interaction, integration, and evolutionary learning experience (IIE) by the property of pervasive inter-variable complementarities. By the evaluation of the well-being function the scientific, economic, and societal moral inclusiveness represented by the holism of treatment and cure of the pandemic is based on complementarities between the good things of life while avoiding the forbidden other. In the present specific case of selection of the relevant vari-ables of life-fulfilling socio-economic development we have selected those specific variables that complement between them in support of sustainabil-ity of the holistic life-fulfilling worldview of wellbeing criterion.

The statistical coefficients of expression (4.7) in its non-linear form, which can be logarithmic in terms of q-induction of all the variables and the coefficients, can be simplified of its extreme complexity in the large system methodical evaluations of the wellbeing function with its endogenous inter-variable system of circular causation relations. Further account is taken of the quantitative form of the wellbeing criterion in terms of the knowledge-based parametric polynomial. Such a polynomial in θ-values may be simpli-fied to its linear form.[16]

Moral inclusiveness of imponderable variables in the wellbeing function and its evaluation

Imponderable variables are the mainstream conceptual and modelling of so-called non-quantifiable variables that are at best treated to convey their exogenous effects. Contrarily, the wellbeing model system (4.1)-(4.6) develops an innovative approach to assigning quantitative parametric val-ues to such variables and endogenizes all the inter-variable relation in their circular causation equations. We formalize this new approach in the following way.

As an example, we write equation (4.1) in its quantitative form as,

$$\theta = A(\theta)\Pi_{k=1}^{10} \, x_k(\theta) \qquad (4.9)$$

included in the **x**-vector are the M-variable and F-variable. All variables are induced by 'θ,' with $0 < \theta < 1$. Let an x_k-variable be the so-called imponder-able variable subject now to its quantification in the wellbeing function and the circular causation equations.

Table 4.1 Evaluating the joint wellbeing function with observed data and imponderables

	1	2	3 ... n_1	evaluated empirical values by CC	Wellbeing S1, S2 Total W
Observable data (Set 1 for observation $i=1,2,..,n_1$)	x_{11}	x_{12}	$x_{13} ... x_{1n1}$	$x'_{11}\ x'_{12}\ x'_{13} ... x'_{1n1}$	θ_1
ordinal values of tabular θ-values for Set 1	θ_{11}	θ_{12}	$\theta_{13} ... \theta_{1n1}$	$\theta'_{11}\ q'_{12}\ \theta'_{13} ... \theta'_{1n1}$	
	1	2	3 ... n_2		$\theta = {}^{n2}\sqrt{\prod_{j=1}{}^{n2}\theta'_{2j}}$
Survey data (Set 2 for survey data $J=1,2,..n_2$)	x_{21}	x_{22}	$x_{23} ... x_{2n2}$	$x'_{21}\ x'_{22}\ x'_{23} ... x'_{2n2}$	$\theta2$
ordinal values of tabular θ values for Set 2	θ_{21}	θ_{22}	$\theta_{23} ... \theta_{2n2}$	$\theta'_{21}\ \theta'_{22}\ \theta'_{23} ... q'_{2n2}$	

In the example of possible data extract in Table 4.1 the total set of data is divided into two segments. Set 1 comprises the observable data. This data set is used to evaluate the wellbeing function $W_1(\theta)$ for data Set 1 along with its entirety of methods using the circular causation and the final empirically evaluated wellbeing function given by say θ_1.

The other segmented data set is gathered by a questionnaire survey. The empirical version of the wellbeing function corresponding to the data Set 2 is likewise entirely evaluated as θ_2. The full theoretical system of circular causation equations (CC), say 'n' in number, is likewise evaluated by the segmented systems of n_1 and n_2 ($n_1 + n_2 = n$) number of equations corresponding to the two separately empirical wellbeing functions, θ_1 and θ_2.

Finally, the joint empirical version of the wellbeing function comprising the observable and the surveyed segments is given by $\theta = \theta_1.\theta_2$, allowing for interaction, integration, and evolutionary learning properties of the total wellbeing function. A weaker IIE-form of the total wellbeing function with such properties would be $\theta = \theta_1 + \theta_2$.

The derivation of θ_2 from the questionnaire survey is straightforward. The Likert responses to the number of questionnaires can be averaged over the number of respondents. These Likert averages point out the importance attached to the specific questionnaires. The resulting averages are then further averaged to obtain the wellbeing index. This version of the wellbeing index can be computed by geometric average of the individual Likert averages by specific questionnaires over numbers of respondents. The geometric computation formula is shown in Table 4.1.

In the detailed empirical evaluation of the wellbeing function 'θ_1' with the system of circular causation equations the algorithmic approach can be used to generate the data points of $\{\theta'_{11}, \theta'_{12}, q'_{13}, \ldots, \theta'_{1n1}\}$. In this case we generate by pro-rata, $\theta'_{1j} = (x_{1j}/x_{1j}*).\theta_{1j}*$; $x_{1j}*$ denotes the most preferred observed variable value for which $\theta_{1j}*$ is assigned the most preferred value. This method of generating evaluated values of $\{\theta'_{1j}\}$ is generalized for the whole data Table 4.1 across (i, j)-values. The value of $\theta_{1j}*$ is of ordinal nature and can be selected by appropriate choice for the whole table of $x(\theta)$-data.

The empirical wellbeing predictor is evaluated for each of the observed $x(\theta)$-variables with data from the Excel-sheet by rows like for the choice of $\theta* = 1$ for x*-values in every column of $x(\theta)$-values. Other ordinal values of $\theta*$ can be similarly selected.

$$[x_1, \theta_1 = x_1/x_1*; x_2, \theta_2 = x_2/x_2*; \ldots; x_{n1}, \theta_{n1} = x_{n1}/x_{n1}*]$$
$$\rightarrow [\theta = \text{Avg}\{\theta_{n1}\}]. \tag{4.10}$$

This computation is repeated over all values by rows of $x(\theta)$-values across columns.

A generalized expression of the wellbeing criterion in unity of pandemic treatments by their scientific, economic, and societal moral inclusiveness

The expressions (4.1)–(4.8) form a generalized system of pandemic treatments and scientific, economic, and societal moral inclusiveness towards attaining normalcy and sustainability. These expressions can be included together in the following schematic Figure 4.3. The figure exhibits the ontological correctness of the multidimensional conception of unity of knowledge underlying its logical formalism. The overarching property of multidisciplinary ensemble and multidimensionality of the generalized logical formalism of the world-system in unity of knowledge establishes the socio-scientific worldview of universality and uniqueness. The pandemic treatments model is one such model. The property of universality is established by the generalized and most extended application of the concept and formalism of the stated model to all categories of pandemic towards attaining normalcy. The property of uniqueness is established by the singular existence of conscious phenomenological inclusiveness in the formal model, unlike its absence in all existing forms of pandemic treatments and curative models to date.

Primal X Ontology	[Socio-Scientific] X Formalism	Phenomenology X (Conscious Inclusiveness)	Continuum (Evolutionary Process-Wise Learning
Unity of Knowledge mutation as manifestation of coronavirus versus deconstruction of mutation to normalcy	deriving socio-scientific logical formalism (Treatment for normalcy by destroying mutation of coronavirus) by wellbeing objective criterion	Application of treatments to gain normalcy out of mutation: coronavirus treatment to normalcy	generalization sustainability

Figure 4.3 A generalized schema of pandemic reversal to normalcy by the model of science-economy-society moral inclusiveness

The nature of the generalized pandemic normalcy model summarized in Figure 4.3 invokes a full list of epistemological explanation. The most important of the epistemic attributes is that such a model denies the axiom of rationality as otherwise is ingrained in mainstream economics (Sen, Summer 1977).[17] By the existence of the axiom of economic rationality in the mainstream model, this genre of utilitarian models ignores the problem of moral inclusiveness. Such a constraint especially denies the study of multidimensional issues with evaluative factors. The problem persists in all of mainstream economic models. The result then is their inability to study science-economy-society morally embedded kind of endogenous circular causation relations. These are otherwise required for algorithmic study of pandemic control towards attaining normalcy by way of the complementarity of endogenous relations of moral inclusiveness between the scientific, economic, and social variables.

Another example of science-economy-society moral inclusiveness: socio-economic development indicators in the wellbeing objective criterion

Indexing millennium development goals (United Nations, 2015)[18]

The millennium development goals (MDGs) are calculated independently of each other by averaging of data within particular domains that are of interest. These variables are 1 poverty alleviation; 2 universal primary education; 3 gender equality; 4 reduction in child mortality; 5 improved maternal health; 6 combat diseases; 7 environmental sustainability; and 8 developing global partnership. The averaging computational approach in these indicators can be seen in the example of measuring poverty gap (PG) in the following way:

$$PG = (1/n)*\Sigma_{i=1}^{q}[(z-y_i)/z] \tag{4.11}$$

Where z denotes poverty line of income;
$\quad$ y_i denotes income of individual 'i';
$\quad$ q denotes number of poor people; and
$\quad$ n denotes size of population.

An alternative way for measuring PG is used:

$$PG = I*H \tag{4.12}$$

Where 'I' denotes income ratio calculated as

$$I = (z-y_q)/z; \text{ with } y_q = (1/q)*\Sigma_{i=1}^{q} y_i. \tag{4.13}$$

$$H \text{ denotes head count ratio calculated as } H = q/n \tag{4.14}$$

It is noted in each of the previously mentioned indexes that the study of socio-economic development by using such averaged indicators does not give the interactive and complex interrelations between critical variables that together define the idea of sustainability. In regard to such complex interrelations of the development paradigm the South Commission Report remarks on the sustainable development worldview. South Commission (1990, p. 13)[19] defines the meaning of socio-economic development in its broad sense encompassing economic, social, and human factors as follows: "To sum up: development is a process of self-reliant growth, achieved through participation of the people acting in their own interests as they see them, and under their own control." The central implication and context of the South Commission's definition of socio-economic development is to construct a vastly relational process for determining what human choices are appropriate within a participatory and codetermined perspective of development. Such a principle is particularly prescribed for the developing countries in view of the potential that they can jointly share in, and can be enacted, to realize justice in the global arrangement of ownership and management of resources towards determining self-reliance. This relational view of dynamic complementarities among the various potential that the developing countries can together render now becomes the premise of a new praxis of development as an organically relational process in respect of the ontology of unity of knowledge. Within this worldview, the interactive and consensual phenomena (integrative) of markets, economies, institutions, and policies assume their nature, formalism, objectives, and viability.

The MDG-indicators are included as complementary inter-causal relations in the wellbeing objective criterion. If now we extend the MDG-indicators into the model of moral inclusiveness issue of socio-economic development in COVID-19 episode, the surest way for such a realization in analytical and ethical equivalence is the extensively complementary perspective. This extension would be across diverse systemic wellbeing quantifications that are then compounded together, as explained in the section comprising Table 4.1. We write this compound quantification in systems $S_i(\theta_i)$ with their individual wellbeing measures, $W_i(S_i(\theta_i))$, in the form of the following compound expression: The wellbeing problem is Evaluation $W(\Pi_i S_i(\theta_i)) = \theta = {}^n\sqrt{\Pi_{i=1}^n\theta_i} = {}^n\sqrt{\Pi P_{i=1}^n(\mathbf{x}_i(\theta))}$, as geometric mean. To a second best this expression can be an additive case. Circular causation equations in the system-specific variables apply. Thereby, we obtain a large number of wellbeing indicators and their induced vectors, with $n = \Sigma_i n_i$ number of equations segmented by the system-specific wellbeing values and their systemic compounding.

Monetary and fiscal effects in the moral and social inclusiveness of millennium index according to the wellbeing objective criterion

It remains to be discussed whether monetary and fiscal effects are purely macroeconomic factors or whether there is a theoretical microeconomic implication underlying macro-micro coordination. The answer to this impending question further penetrates into that of micro-money (Choudhury, 2018)[20] and to the more bewildering issue of whether there really is a macroeconomic field that is embedded in microeconomic foundations and capable of the study of moral inclusiveness. The answer to this deeply theoretical query is much more than simply that covered by the field of microfoundation of macroeconomics (Phelps, 1970).[21]

First, to answer the question of the exclusive nature of ethico-economics, the entire study of the economic problem is vested with its embedding of moral inclusiveness in microeconomics. There exist no aggregation of microeconomic preferences, microeconomic aggregation of variables, and decision-making transcending microeconomics to macroeconomics. Thereby, ethical variables, which are microeconomic entities, cannot be transferred into macroeconomics. The theoretical derivation of the model of science-economy-society moral inclusiveness for addressing the pandemic problem in generalized terms is of a distinctly different genre. Neither the existing microeconomic nor macroeconomic conceptual mould is adequate to address the multidimensional issues of the pandemic episode.

Yet again, even though preferences and choices of ethical types are to be found in microeconomics they are exogenously datum in nature. Consequently endogenous ethical preferences and variables cannot be found in any sort of science-economy-society complementarities in macroeconomics. Thus all of the interactive, integrative, and evolutionary learning dynamics of the inter-systemic complementary nature in the learning socio-economic world-system does not exist in either mainstream microeconomics or macroeconomics and in science and social studies as endogenous factors. The end result is that an economy-wide concept with its ethico-economic description abides in the economy-wide sense of knowledge-induced complementarities in the wellbeing context with a distinctive conception. It does not exist either in mainstream microeconomics or macroeconomics.

In the ethico-economic theory, its model and application as a whole, and with money and fiscal factors converge into their endogenous forms pertaining to the model of science-economy-society-wide moral inclusiveness as explained by inter-variable circular causation complementarities between the variables of the wellbeing function as objective criterion. Thereby, in this kind of endogenous science-economy-society-wide transformation, money and fiscal variables assume their complementary coordination with the ethical meaning of organic pairing. This pervasive complementary properties of money and fiscal variables as endogenous variables and in regard to all other variables overarching the science, economic, and social sides have the singular meaning of ethical, social, and moral inclusiveness relations in respect of economic and other multidimensional general evolutionary equilibrium convergences. Such a theoretical construct relating to scientific, economic, and moral inclusiveness is not found and cannot be misconstrued with the existing theory of micro-foundation of macroeconomics, based as this area is in the neoclassical treatment of preferences and the axiom of economic rationality. Such properties do not conform with the socio-scientific epistemic theory of unity of knowledge with its IIE-learning properties in the generalized model of wellbeing with materiality and ethics as morally inclusive choices at the exclusion of contrary ones.

Conclusion

This chapter has formalized an ontological and applied model of a unique nature that is different from mainstream socio-economic understanding. The systemically formalized epistemic nature of the imminent model 'treats' all forms of the pandemic problems by unifying the observed and imponderable sets of variables and their critical relations. All such entities interact, integrate, and endogenously learn by evolution in unity of knowledge as the ontological principle derived from the methodological worldview of the Qur'an. Within the categories of the interrelated variables of the scientific, economic, social, and the imponderable types focusing on the comprehensive socio-economic development by stemming the tide of pandemic effects, the three critical sets of variables studied are as follows in this chapter. They are money, fiscal, and other endogenous socio-economic variables induced by knowledge and attribute parameters. The $\theta(\varepsilon)$-induced variables are shown to play their interactive, integrative, and evolutionary learning roles of sustainability based on the episteme of unity of knowledge as substantively defined.

Monetary, fiscal, and socio-economic variables including the observed and the imponderable ones are all endogenously related via circular causation. Thereby, the policy instruments connected with these variables are also endogenous and circular causal in nature. The consequential over-encompassing entirety of interactive, integrative, and evolutionary learning (IIE) variables as endogenously interrelated point out the consciousness of individual, collective, national, and global responsible behavioural conduct beyond simply the mechanical type of socio-scientific nature.

The endogenous nature of money, fiscal spending, and their policy variables imply that their expansionary or contractionary forms are interactively and consensually determined by continuous discourse between the public and private participants. Thereby, in their resulting participatory decision-making framework, as in the case of global monetary and fiscal implementation, the conscious preferences and behavioural conduct bring about collective moral consensus. The consequence thereby is a mitigation of transaction costs caused otherwise by the political economy and the inter-regional disagreements on models of global monetary and fiscal responsibilities. There are the profound theoretical discoveries along with their applications of treating endogenous moral and ethical inclusiveness in a comprehensive materiality and behavioural model for sustainable treatment of generalized forms of pandemic problems. There is also the rise of the material and moral inclusiveness by way of extensively participatory relations between science, socio-economic, societal, and human interactions extending over intra- and inter-systems.

Equations (4.7) and (4.8) in policy terms signified by percentage rates of monetary, fiscal, and socio-economic materiality and imponderable variables convey the following effects on comprehensive treatments of pandemic with material and moral inclusiveness by virtue of their complementarities: First, monetary and fiscal complementarities are induced by θ-values over sustainable cycles of evolutionary learning causing sustainability in

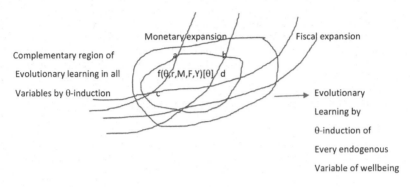

Figure 4.4 Complementary expansion of {θ,M,F,Y,r}[θ] in the evolutionary
θ-induced region of a,b,c,d

continuum of knowledge, space, and time, all induced by unity of knowledge. Second, the θ-induced socio-economic and imponderable variables are jointly affected by the positive monetary and fiscal complementarities of moral inclusiveness.

Figure 4.4 shows the simultaneous monotonic positive interrelations of the variables in the vector {θ,M,F,Y,r}[θ] under the sustainable impact of evolutionary learning by {θ(ε)}. The vector of variable 'r(θ)' denotes rates of return in all the variables caused by their complementarities in the multidimensional world-system of wellbeing by pandemic treatments with science-economy-society moral inclusiveness. Now there is no meaning in placing axes of reference in Figure 4.4 because complementary θ-induction in the continuum of {θ,M,F,Y,r}[θ] causes such endogenous inter-variable circular causal relations and their coefficients to be of non-Cartesian nature. In this form the complementarities of variables of science-economy-society moral inclusiveness are explainable by non-linear and complex topological mathematics (Maddox, 1971; Bertuglia & Vaio, 2005).[22]

Notes

1 Nicolau, E. (1995). "Cybernetics: The bridge between divided knowledge and interdisciplinarity", *Kybernetes: International Journal of Systems and Cybernetics*, 24:7, pp. 21–25.
2 Lan, J.A. (2020). "Small connections between course material and everyday life pop up all the time, in almost any course I teach in my field", in *Coping with Coronavirus*, The Chronicle of Higher Education. Lan writes: "If we want students to develop expertise in our fields, then, we have to help them thicken up the connections – from the first week of the semester to the fifth, from the last

course they took in our discipline to this one, from the course material to their lives outside of class. The more connections they can create, the more they can begin to formulate their own ideas and gain a wider view of our fields."

3 Bergoc, J.N. & Andolsek, D.M. (2019). *Ethical Infrastructure, the Road to Moral Management*, Cambridge Scholars Publishing, New Castle upon Tyne.

4 Dreyfus, H.L. & Rabinow, P., trans. (1983). *M. Foucault: Beyond Structuralism and Hermeneutics, the Archeology of the Human Sciences*, University of Chicago Press, Chicago, IL.

5 Veblen, T. (1899 (1912). "Conspicuous consumption", in *The Theory of the Leisure Class*, The Macmillan Co., New York.

6 Inglott, P.S. (1990). "The rights of future generations: Some socio-philosophical considerations", in S. Busuttil, E. Agius, P.S. Inglott & T. Macelli, eds. *Our Responsibilities Towards Future Generations*, pp. 17–27, Foundation for International Studies & UNESCO, Malta.

7 Linda Villarosa Photographs by Kasimu Harris, L. (May 20, 2020). "'A terrible price': The deadly racial disparities of Covid-19 in America", *The New York Times Magazine*; X_3.

8 Levine, D. (1988). *Needs, Rights, and the Market*, Lynne Reiner, Boulder, CO.

9 Hawley, A. (1986). *Human Ecology, a Theoretical Essay*, University of Chicago Press, Chicago, IL.

10 Holton, R.J. (1992). "Defining the economy: A historical, multi-dimensional approach", in his *Economy and Society*, pp. 7–22, Routledge, London.

11 Streeten, P. (2014). *Development Perspectives*, Palgrave Macmillan, Basingstoke, London.

12 The IIE dynamics that characterize the knowledge-induction of all the variables of $\mathbf{Z}(\theta)$ are explained in Figure 2. In this figure the central intersected domain denotes the integrated result of interactive relations shown by the expanding circles, which also explains the simultaneous effect of the evolutionary learning multidisciplinary S-domains. The IIE dynamics of knowledge-induced consequences are summarized as follows:
$(d/d\theta)[\cup^{\text{interaction}} \cap^{\text{integration}} W(\mathbf{Z}(\theta))] > 0$.

13 Partial elasticity coefficients are defined as follows: for a specific circular causation equation, $\ln x_i(\theta) = a_0 + \Sigma_j a_j.\ln x_j(\theta)$, partial elasticity coefficient of $x_i(\theta)$ to $x_j(\theta)$ is defined as, $\partial \ln x_i(\theta)/\partial \ln x_j(\theta) = [\partial \ln x_i(\theta)/\partial \theta]/[\partial \ln x_j(\theta)/\partial \theta] = [x_j(\theta)/x_i(\theta)]*[\partial x_i(\theta)/\partial x_j(\theta)] = \in_{i,j}(\theta)$, i,j=1,2, . . .

14 Mankiw, G. (2016). *Macroeconomics*, Worth Publishers, New York. Note how the monetary and fiscal policy impacts work: $d\ln M/d\ln Y = (Y/M)*(dM/dY) > 0$, for by monetary theory, $dM/dY > 0$. Likewise, $\partial \ln f_1/\partial \ln F = (F/M)*(\partial M/\partial F) > 0$. The other inter-variable relations also imply their positivity.

15 Stanford Encyclopedia of Philosophy. (2016). *Capability Approach*.

16 The polynomial form of 'θ' and θ-induced coefficients wellbeing function, $W(\theta)$, is, $W(\theta) = a_0(\theta)+a_1(\theta)*\theta+a_2(\theta)*\theta^2+ \ldots$. That is, $[W(\theta)-a_0(\theta)] = \Phi(\theta)$ to a linear approximation of θ, and hence of $F(\theta)$, with $0 < \theta < 1$. Therefore also, $0 < \Phi(\theta) < 1$. Thus to a linear approximation in 'θ' and 'Φ' we can write the wellbeing function in its scalar differential form as, $[(W(\theta) - a_0(\theta))] = \Phi(\theta)$. The following theorem now applies: A monotonic positive transformation of a utility function (now wellbeing function) is a utility function (hence wellbeing function). Henderson, J.M. & Quandt, R.E. (1971). *Microeconomic Theory, a Mathematical Approach*, McGraw-Hill, New York, NY.

17 Sen, A.K. (Summer, 1977). "Rational fools: A critique of the behavioral foundations of economic theory", *Philosophy & Public Affairs*, 6:4, pp. 317–344.
18 United Nations. (2015). *Millennium Development Goals Report*, New York.
19 South Commission. (1990). *The Challenge to the South*, Oxford University
Press, Oxford.
20 Choudhury, M.A. (2018). "Micro-money, finance, and real economy interrelationship in the framework of Islamic ontology of unity of knowledge and the
world-system of social economy", *International Journal of Social Economics*,
45:2.
21 Phelps, E.S. (1970). "The new microeconomics in employment and inflation
theory", in E.S. Phelps et al., eds. *Microeconomic Foundations of Employment
and Inflation Theory*, pp. 1–27, W.W. Norton, New York.
22 Maddox, I.J. (1971). *Functional Analysis*, Cambridge University Press,
Cambridge.
Bertuglia, C.S. & Vaio, F. (2005). "Dynamical systems and the phase space", in
their *Non-Linearity, Chaos & Complexity, the Dynamics of Natural and Social
Systems*, pp. 49–70, Oxford University Press, Oxford.

5 A generalized model of science-economy-society moral inclusiveness in complex pandemic regime

Introduction

A mathematical theory of evolutionary learning process that can represent a universal and unique model to study issues and problems spanning all disciplines is unknown in existing socio-scientific studies. This existing state of affairs in socio-scientific methodology is contrary to the permanent existence of an epistemic worldview of unity of knowledge in understanding soul-mind-matter organic interrelations. A theory of socio-scientific system, namely of 'everything' that organically explains unification in and between the social and natural sciences by the episteme of unity of knowledge is present to a degree in the natural sciences. But it is absent in political economy, economics, and the social sciences.

The modelling and analysis of complexly evolutionary learning systems that are epistemologically driven by unity of knowledge present non-linear dynamics. A theory of process-oriented modelling in non-linear evolutionary learning spaces underlying economy, science, and society interrelationship is formalized in this chapter.

An implication of empirical work illustrates the treatment of non-linear problems in modelling the interrelations between knowledge-induced interactive variables. The influence of organic relationship characterizing each variable in terms of the other ones is formalized. Non-linearity in such complex knowledge-induced interaction is exhibited either by evolutionary equilibrium or by disequilibrium, as the case may be between convergence to normalcy or mutation, respectively. The empirical method that emerges is referred to as circular causation between the variables of interactive and integrative evolutionary learning process model. We explain this aspect of non-linearity by modelling the interrelationship between economic growth rate, poverty rate, and wellbeing. The substantive concept of wellbeing is defined by means of the objectified organic relations that ought to be explained normatively by circular causal relations between the variables following the inductive nature of the prevailing state of complexity.

This chapter is largely a reproduction of the published paper (Choudhury, Mariyanti & Hossain, 2014).[1] Its objective is to point out the complex and non-linear nature of the science-economy-society model of moral inclusiveness. Such a creative model is found to be appropriate for application to the study of pandemic treatments, cure, and normalization. The underlying rationale for selecting such a model for studying the complex pandemic problem is the need for establishing an abstracto-empirical rigorously analytical model of science-economy-society-wide moral inclusiveness. The model formalized for the study of pandemic regime is derived on ontological foundations followed by its wellbeing perspective of application and sustainability.

Background

Socio-scientific models to date have sparsely matured in the area encompassing the broader explanation of knowledge-embedded social processes and events. A remarkable exception is the viewpoint of Hayek's (1945)[2] and Myrdal's (1958)[3] knowledge-embedded systems are characterized by the complexity of system-dynamics concerning the variables that represent the complexity of the knowledge-induced sub-systems. Instead, socio-scientific modelling has proceeded on as an isolated nicety within its own niche of specialization, but at the loss of social realism. Mathematics and statistics have thus continued on to be used in economic modelling in isolation of the greater outlook of social, cultural, and multifaceted decision-making processes (Beed & Kane, 1991).[4] These together characterize socio-scientific interaction. This kind of deepening academic development in socio-scientific studies have been to the detriment of studying and enriching the field of credible prediction of the events as we experience them (Soros, 1998).[5]

Yet the system modelling and inferences gained in the field of knowledge-embedded system, being overarched across sub-systems of the human entirety, reflects a semblance of methodological universality of such broader formalism of modelling. And if the field of such overarching extensions across multidisciplinary sub-systems expands, the emerging models are likely to converge into uniqueness of the modelling enterprise by their capability for higher dimensional analysis. Boland (1991)[6] writes in this regard that a higher level of falsification possibility of a theory may supplant a lower-level criticizability. Such a conjectural aspect of episteme and modelling would comprise ever-expanding domains of universality of emergent theories over previously conceptualized ones (Popper, 1998).[7]

Future of socio-scientific modelling

The formalism on convergence to a universal and unique theory in all the sciences is a project of realizing a universal and unique model that can answer the nature of scientific arguments in general in 'everything' (Barrow, 1991)[8] and in the derived particulars of the general-system modelling. This course of research invites a burst of diverse issues and problems that are specific to different disciplines yet are embedded in the generality of interactive system. But they are all capable of studying by the self-same model of socio-scientific investigation. Thus, we coin the term "the socio-scientific" to represent the holistic systemic worldview of integrated science and society. Within this lies economics as social science.

As well, since universality and uniqueness of such a model applies to all issues and problems across diverse disciplines the modelling enterprise implies the epistemology of unity of knowledge between the diversely emergent categories of issues, problems, and disciplines. The resulting theory of the socio-scientific 'everything' now combines a new substantive theory of the social sciences and the natural sciences together in one intellectual enterprise. The organic linkage and explanation of concepts and implications emanating from the application of the unique and universal model has its methodology premised on the epistemology of unity of knowledge to study the dynamics of organically unified systems. These by their fuzzy space of lack of determinateness reflect non-linear relations.

With such extensions of the modelling enterprise the aspects of the overarching exercise combined with its emerging character of universality and uniqueness in studying the organic unity and process orientation of the embedded sub-systems bring forth the investigation of the embedded social political economy. The corresponding theory of such a process-oriented extensively systemic study as social political economy yields a study of political economy that is different from the received one. Now the traditional definition of political economy ceases to be simply the study of differentiated and disequilibrium dynamics of competing agency and power in ownership, production, and distribution of wealth and resources (George, 1897)[9] between opposing agents in economy and society.

The field of social political economy is different. Its interactive field of diverse phenomena appropriately characterizes the pandemic regime. Social political economy as embedded socio-scientific system of interactions is understood as the epistemological study of multitudes of organically unifying sub-systems of the human order. The forces underlying the meeting grounds of interaction between such systems show conflict by marginalism between competing opposites. Interaction, integration, and organically relational unification remain absent (Sztompka, 1991).[10] When conflicts exist the epistemological groundwork of unity of knowledge between the 'de-knowledge'-induced multivariate sub-systems denotes an opposite state to moral and ethical field. Such a state of the inter-variables requires moral reconstruction. Thereby, the positivistic nature of the evaluated 'de-knowledge' situation becomes an unwanted situation of conflicts and differentiation. This state represents a socio-scientific nature of opposite complementarities and methodological individualism as singularity between the variables and 'de-knowledge'-induced systems.

Non-linearity underlying reconstruction of the 'de-knowledge' state of socio-scientific modelling to the framework of knowledge-induced system modelling bears the properties of interaction leading to integration and then to evolutionary epistemology by intra- and inter-systemic dynamics. In the re-modelled case of knowledge-induction the reconstructed socio-scientific modelling gets premised in the episteme of unity of knowledge. These properties of the reconstructed 'de-knowledge' socio-scientific model revert into the knowledge-induced socio-scientific model. It is then accordingly transformed into the model of moral inclusiveness with its econometric properties of predictability and controllability. The transformed sub-systems now establish complementarities in the sense of system-ensemble. The entire evaluation of the wellbeing function conveys analytical consequences that are premised on the epistemological worldview of the unified socio-scientific whole.

Now evolution as history of the future of system-ensemble and a fresh way of understanding the pandemic socio-scientific ensemble represents a reconstructed possibility of sustainability driven by the epistemological nature of organic unity of multidisciplinary systems. We explain such extensively organic unity of relations in terms of pervasive complementarities between the variables and agencies of the embedded sub-systems. The principle of pervasive complementarities in multidisciplinary embedding of the scientific, economic, social, and other forces is equivalent to having intra-systemic and inter-systemic participation between agents, agencies, and their characterizing variables (Choudhury, 2007).[11] Such a multidisciplinary ensemble of diversity of the socio-scientific reconstruction establishes the model of holistic moral inclusiveness.

Objective

In this chapter we introduce this substantive area of new research of systemic interaction, integration, and evolutionary dynamics driven by the epistemic worldview of unity of knowledge. This episteme overarches across economy, science, and society interrelations in the context of moral inclusiveness embodying the wellbeing objective criterion. The underlying properties all the more form the complexity of a pandemic episode. The epistemological groundwork of such organic interrelations is based on unity of systemic knowledge. It addresses the phenomenon of organic linkages between multidisciplinary areas overarching all issues and problems that are represented by selected multidisciplinary system-variables interconnecting the systemic relations. Here first, deductive reasoning leads into inductive analytics. In continuation inductive reasoning subsequently re-emerges as deductive continuity of learning across processes of organic unity of knowledge. The governing worldview of unity of knowledge in non-linear and complex learning dynamics is required to endow the emergent processes with sustained predictability and controllability. The emergent modelling of science-economy-society moral inclusiveness of treatment, curative, and their sustainability presented in this work forms the altogether fresh overview of the moral ensemble along with the cognitive field of materiality that embodies the mechanical part of the holistic model of science-economy-society moral inclusion.

Explanation

The inherent systemically unified methodology expresses two kinds of participative organic unity of being and becoming (Prigogine, 1980).[12] First, there is the inner dynamics of interaction within sub-systems. This leads into integration (convergence). Interaction leading to integration continues on to evolutionary equilibrium. Thus IIE-process dynamics sustain in learning processes. Such interactive, integrative, and evolutionary (IIE) dynamics appear and melt away in learning processes within and across the multidiscipline ensemble in reference to the holistic approach to investigating the problems under study. All these properties comprise intra-system dynamics and both characterize and apply to pandemic problems. Second, simultaneously by continuous mathematical functionals there comes about evolution of the interactive and integrative processes into new phases of evolutionary learning intra- and inter-systems (Whitehead, 1978).[13] Such emergent processes are referred to as evolutionary learning processes inter-systems.

The resulting organically unifying phases within any learning process are thereby universalized and remain unique in the interdependent socio-scientific issues by the dynamics of interaction leading to integration, and thereby to evolution (IIE). Such dynamics occur continuously in phases of learning and repetition of the same kind of causal functional relations between the multivariates and their circular causation relations.

Knowledge arising from the systemic understanding of embedded subsystemic interrelations becomes the foundational force of consequences and change. While knowledge is epistemic in nature relating to the system-ensemble concept (Hubner, 1985),[14] its degree of incidence to form organic unity of knowledge-embedded interrelated systems is evaluated by positivistic methods of analysis. The estimated results point out the normative futures to be constructed as opposed to the socially unwanted estimated ones.

In such evolutionary learning dynamics of embedded sub-systems, 'time' enters in a peculiar way. Time *does not cause* change or reconstruction. Thereby, the science-economy-society moral inclusiveness in pandemic treatment and cure is benign of its occurrence and disappearance by the depth of consciousness of moral inclusiveness. In this respect 'time' simply plays the deterministic role of recording events and evaluations. Yet in the IIE-process methodology any state of the socio-scientific system is evolved into newer ones by knowledge-flows that are endogenously generated and continued on in the IIE-learning processes over time. 'Events' by definition are thereby a concrescence of knowledge induction in space and time. Consequences of the recurrent 'events,' as by socio-scientific valuations, actualize in knowledge, space, and time dimensions (Choudhury, 2009).[15]

All events in such an epistemic framework of learning dynamics are probabilistic in nature, spanning the self-same pattern of circular causality between knowledge-embedded systems. Thereby, there arise extensively complementary organic relations between the variables representing sub-systems. All variables are driven by knowledge-flows. Hence, they remain endogenous in relations interrelating sub-systems by the IIE-evolutionary learning processes.

A brief review of the literature in the thematic field of embedded system modelling pertaining to pandemic regime of treatment and cure

In this brief section (see Choudhury & Hossain, 2007 for an extensive coverage)[16] we point out a search for formalism along the type of IIE-modelling. The emergent non-linear models generate perturbations caused by the multidisciplinary nature and the inherent complex aggregation that emerge (Bertuglia & Vaio, 2005).[17] Mathematical functionals of non-linear topological spaces arise (Kupka & Peixoto, 1993).[18]

Such inferences on the nature of non-linear modelling that emerge by systemic knowledge-embedding go beyond Chichilnisky (1990),[19] Gel'fand & Shenitzer (1961),[20] and Debreu (1990)[21] treatments of topological systems. But the idea of complex aggregation of topological cells into higher dimensional manifolds of ensemble was started by Smale (1990).[22] The multilinear economic relations forming tensor variations of the coefficients of the manifold functionals is referred to as 'foliation.' They also represent the science-economy-society moral ensemble, that is moral inclusiveness for the study of pandemic causes, treatment, and curative modelling.

In the end the normative study of reconstructed systems is made amenable to complex events in interactive sub-systems. Consequently convexity of optimal surfaces and the assumptions of perfectly competitive markets, and steady-state equilibrium together with the 'objective' postulate of optimization, cannot mark the field of such mathematical applications in socio-scientific theory. On the other hand, linearity of the mathematical equations that characterize all of mathematical applications as in econometrics is due to the parametric constant or assumed patterns of probabilistic variations in estimated coefficients. At best, assumed Bayesian probability distributions are assigned to the estimated coefficients. In pandemic ensemble of moral inclusiveness all variables and parameters learn continuously by the consciousness caused by interaction, integration, and evolutionary learning of entities in multidisciplinary ensemble.

Contrary to the linear approach inter-system complexity caused by knowledge-embedding and foliation is exhibited by the learning values of the 'simulated' coefficients of the model. The estimated coefficients are probabilistic in nature. But the probability distribution function of the coefficients in the case of modelling sub-systemic knowledge-embedding is determined not by pre-assignment, such as by normal distribution. Rather, the probability distribution of 'simulated' coefficients in the IIE-process models of intra- and inter-systemic knowledge-embedding is determined by the prevalent socio-scientific states in which the organic relations appear in any sub-systemic embedding by knowledge-induction.

IIE-model formalism in non-linear topological space

We construct here the salient features of the evolutionary learning process model in Figure 5.1. By the recursive effect (circular causation) of interaction and integration between the variables (Myrdal, 1958)[23] ($x_1(\theta)$, $x_2(\theta)$) by way of f_1 and $\beta.f_1^{-1}$; f_2 and $\alpha.f_2^{-1}$, an evaluation functional follows. It is referred to as the wellbeing function by virtue of its descriptive functional based on unity of knowledge. The knowledge-flow variables determined in terms of the foundational episteme of unity of knowledge is the assigned θ-value. See the illustrative method of assignment of such q-values in this work in terms of the socio-scientific variables under study by the wellbeing concept. The imminent methodology with its analytics is universally applicable to all forms of issues of moral inclusiveness in diverse system ensemble. The pandemic case is just an exemplar of its broadest episteme and application.

The wellbeing function is the evaluative criterion that normatively yet quantitatively measures degrees of 'estimated' and 'simulated' complementarities that are possible between the selected variables. Such degrees of complementarities represent the epistemic sign of participatory interrelationship between the selected variables. The degrees of positivistic estimated and normatively simulated complementarities are empirically set on the basis of given data. The 'estimated' circular causation equations are next simulated by assigning new values to the estimated coefficients reflecting normative change in the light of systemic unity of knowledge. Such simulated functionals are denoted by g_1 and g_2 in Figure 5.1. There are as many circular causation relations as there are variables in the wellbeing function, and thereby, in the generalized state of the ensemble. The circular causation system of relations is thus uniquely solvable for any set of assigned predictor values of the variables consequential to simulation.

The wellbeing functional criterion that is simulated by the recursive relations intra-system (i.e. in a single process) is formally denoted by $W(x_1(\theta), x_2(\theta))$. The recursive relations, i.e. the circular causation equations to estimate and simulate the circular causation relations between the variables are the following ones:

$$x_1 = f_1(x_2(\theta), \theta); \ x_2 = f_2(x_1(\theta), \theta); \tag{5.1}$$
and the recursively generated knowledge-value given by,
$$\theta = G(x_1(\theta), x_2(\theta)). \tag{5.2}$$
$$i = 1, 2$$

Note that since the simulated θ-function shown by $G(..)$ is a monotonic positive empirical representation of the wellbeing index, therefore, $\theta = G(x_1(\theta), x_2(\theta))$ is a similar functional representation of $W(x_1(\theta), x_2(\theta))$. Thus, the measured $\theta \equiv W(.) = G(..)$ represents the 'measurable' objective functional of wellbeing. The ordinal assignment of θ-values is computed as ranked ordinal numbers. Such ordinal ranks are derived by noting the trends in the $(x_1(\theta), x_2(\theta))$- vector values by virtue of the need for complementarities between them. Such complementarities are read off in reference to the episteme of unity of knowledge as the ethical consequence of organic relationship between the knowledge-induced variables.

Next, evolutionary organic relations cause new knowledge-values to continue across processes of learning as explained by estimation followed by simulation appear continuously. Such emergent evolutionary learning processes are re-originated by new evolutionary inter-systemic θ-values, etc. in the following way:

A completed process intra-system is denoted by:

$$[\theta \rightarrow (x_1(\theta), x_2(\theta)) \rightarrow \text{Simulated } W(x_1(\theta), x_2(\theta)), \tag{5.3}$$

$$\text{subject to } x_1 = f_1(x_2(\theta), \theta); \; x_2 = f_2(x_1(\theta), \theta). \tag{5.4}$$

$$\theta = G(x_1(\theta), x_2(\theta)) \text{ reflects } W(x_1(\theta), x_2(\theta))]. \tag{5.5}$$

The end of a process is followed by the evolution of new θ-value, etc. Note that intra-system (processes) recursive θ-values represent simulated wellbeing indexes by improvement of the estimated coefficient values in reference to actual $(x_1(\theta), x_2(\theta))$ and simulated vector, say the vector-values, $(x_1*(\theta), x_2*(\theta))$. On the other hand, evolutionary θ-values across processes (inter-systems) represent continuous recursive learning over the dimensions of knowledge, space, and time.

Non-linear transforms

The monotonic positive mappings, say F_i, across repetitively interactive, integrative, and evolutionary (IIE-processes) intra-systems and inter-systems of moral inclusiveness denoted by 'i' preserve the self-same kind of IIE-learning processes along with their circular causation mappings for evaluating wellbeing. Yet they do not necessarily converge to the identity mapping. That is recursion of knowledge does not form *linear* mappings. *Non-linearity* of the functional relations (mappings) between the variables remain permanent by the induction of knowledge-flows ($\{\theta\}$)-values.

Thereby, we can write the following results with all forms of compound mappings:

$$F_i \, \text{of}_2^{-1} = F_i \, o\alpha.I = \alpha'.I. \tag{5.6}$$

F_i here denotes arbitrary mappings of the f-functions at the ith round of IIE within a given learning (recursive) process. α' is scalar to indicate non-linear mappings. It is therefore a function of ($\{q\}$)-values in the evaluation of wellbeing function.

$$\text{Likewise, } F_i \, \text{of}_2 = F_i \, o\beta.I = \beta'.I. \tag{5.7}$$

β' are compounded scalar functional of ($\{\theta\}$)-values on β carrying the implication like α' scalar.

$$F_i \, \text{of}_4 = F_i \, o\gamma \, I = \gamma'.I. \tag{5.8}$$

γ' are compounded scalar functional of ($\{\theta\}$)-values on γ.

It is likewise the same kinds of recursive mappings for chains of mappings along the IIE-learning processes. Figures 5.1 and 5.2 can then be extended by indefinitely many integrated mappings explaining as many interrelations as there are emergent variables in the compound maps.

For inter-system learning following evaluation of W(.), the results will be as follows: $F_i(W)$ is a monotonic positive transformation of W(.) by the positive mapping F_i in the ith IIE-simulation process. Thus, $F_i(f_1) = F_i(x_1(\theta))$ represent simulated forms of the estimated functional of $x_1 = f_1(x_2(\theta),\theta)$. $F_i(f_1)$ as arbitrary monotonic positive transformation is recursively set by the simulated θ-value in the ith round of IIE-learning process. $F_i(.)$ thus denotes simulacra of non-linear transforms (Fitzpatrick, 2003; Wallerstein, 1998)[24] with i = 1,2, . . .,n. .

F_i are non-linear by virtue of the density of $\{\theta\}$-values in its ith simulated set of variables. That is,

$$\text{plim}\{\theta\} = \theta^* + \varepsilon(\theta), \tag{5.9}$$
$$d\varepsilon(\theta)/d\theta > 0, \tag{5.10}$$

defining evolutionary equilibriums (Grandmont, 1989; Burstein, 1991).[25]

It can be readily shown by a diagram with θ on the vertical axis and socio-scientific variable on the horizontal axes that the area under the non-linear surface with $\{\text{plim}\{\theta\}\}$ will include all the sequences of $\{\text{plim}\{\theta\}\}$ under the linear surface; but not vice versa. Consequently, the positive non-linear transformation above the linear domain of learning will yield higher vector-values of $\{x_1(\theta,x_2(\theta),\theta\}$. Consequently, $F_i(W(x_1(\theta, x_2(\theta))))_{\text{non-linear learning}} >$ $F_i(W(x_1(\theta,x_2(\theta))))_{\text{linear learning}}$, for $\theta_{\text{non-linear}} > \theta_{\text{linear}}$. Linear transformations form deconstruction of non-linear functional.

By virtue of the positive monotonic transformation of the IIE-learning processes the sets $\{x(\theta)\} = \{(x_1(\theta,x_2(\theta),\theta)\}$, $\{W(\theta)\} = \{W(x_1(\theta), x_2(\theta))\}$, $\{F(x(\theta),\theta)\} = \{F_i(W(x_1(\theta),x_2(\theta)))\}$ and their more elementary functionals form topologies. This is proved simply by noting that the continuously differentiable functionals establish neighbourhood evolutionary learning points intra- and inter-systems. This implies that $\cap\{x(\theta)\} \neq \phi$. Thereby, by the property of continuous positive monotonic transformation, $\cap\{W(\theta)\} \neq \phi$; $\cap\{F(x(\theta),\theta)\} \neq \phi$. Also, in the open learning space of evolutionary $\{\theta\}$-values, any of the mathematical intersections and unions of the given class of sets form similar classes in the learning domain.

Consequently, there are positive monotonic mappings that preserve the nature of the transformations. In the open space of set-theoretic unions and intersections, the universal set of all possible positive monotonic transformations form the universal set of all non-linear possibilities. Such a domain of solutions is referred to as the space of socio-scientific 'everything.'

Finally, the higher density of the non-linear functionals implies that linear spaces appear as exceptions everywhere and in 'everything.' The study of pandemic multidimensional complexity while rearing it towards treatment and cure is just one example. The underlying models of such multidimensional study ensembles can therefore be contained in a set of finite measure, leaving the rest of the complex set of non-linear functionals mathematically 'measurable almost everywhere' – Æ (Friedman, 1982).[26] Thereby, the null-set ϕ separates the space of non-linear mappings from the space of linear mappings. Then by the positive monotonic transformation, the space of non-linear mappings remains above the space of linear mappings – at a higher level of the dimensions of knowledge, time, and space. In this way, the definition of topology as a mapping that preserves these properties of mappings is established (Maddox, 1970).[27]

Yet the topology we have described here is on the domain of non-linear mappings $\{F_i\}$ appearing as compounding, shown by 'o,' of non-linear functionals (shown earlier). Besides, since $\{F_i\}$ explain simulations out of simulacra of changes in the coefficients of the functionals such as $\{f's\}$ and $\{F_i\}$, therefore, every such functional transformation has probabilistic coefficients that are subject to variations continuously.[28] This makes the simulated mappings $\{F_i(f's)\}$ non-linear 'foliation' of 'simulation' relations (shown by the simulated version of the estimated coefficients – predictor coefficient values). In mathematical tensor language the evolutionary learning spaces define unions of evolutionary learning spaces. Such set-theoretic unions signify linear aggregation of non-linear relations caused by simulated relations in terms of knowledge-induced dynamic coefficients (continuous variations by simulated predictor values) and their non-linear specifications of the elementary functions of the compound maps.

Now Figure 5.1 assumes the dynamics shown in Figure 5.2.

Figures 5.1 and 5.2 also explain how the domains of knowledge-induced wellbeing ($W(\theta)$) and 'de-knowledge'-induced mutation functions ($W'(\theta')$) between the treatments towards normalcy and pandemic variables, respectively, remain differentiated in the IIE-learning perspective. The reversed functions like the f's and F's shown in the Figures 5.1 and 5.2 can be expressed in terms the two W-functions as,

$W(\theta)^\alpha \cdot W'(\theta')^\beta = 1$. (α, β) are oppositely assigned positive coefficients of the normalcy and mutation states of pandemic, respectively.

The differentiated domains of pandemic normalcy and mutation through the continuous process of learning implies, $(d/d\theta)[\alpha.\log W(\theta) + \beta.\log W'(\theta')] \approx 0$. This denotes

$$\alpha.(1/W(\theta))*(dW(\theta)/d\theta) + \beta.(1/W'(\theta'))(dW'(\theta')/d\theta')*(d\theta'/d\theta)]$$
$$= \alpha.\in_{W(\theta)|\theta} +\beta.\in_{W'(\theta')|\theta'})*(d\theta'/d\theta) \approx 0. \qquad (5.11)$$

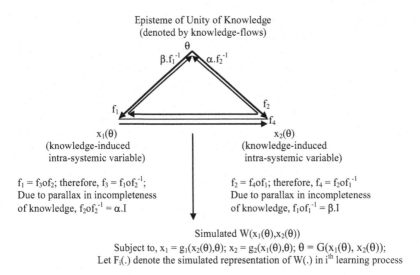

Figure 5.1 The intra-systemic IIE-learning process dynamics

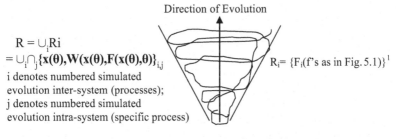

$R_1 = \{F_1(f\text{'s as in Fig.} 5.1)\}$
Each region R_i has a relational triangle as in Fig. 5.1.

Figure 5.2 Evolutionary learning dynamics in non-linear spaces

Expression (5.11) is proved by the fact that $\alpha.\in_{W(\theta)|\theta} > 0$; $b.\in_{W'(\theta')|\theta'}) > 0$; $(d\theta'/d\theta) < 0$ with monotonicity between the wellbeing (dis-wellbeing by de-knowledge) and the respective knowledge (de-knowledge) parameters. The IIE-learning and optimal pandemic states between normalcy and mutation depend upon the values of the elasticity coefficients as shown. This also implies the effectiveness of the change in pandemic normalcy caused by the percentage change in the wellbeing function oppositely to the condition of mutation caused by the percentage change in the dis-wellbeing function of pandemic mutation. Expression (5.11) applies to multidisciplinary ensemble but with the normalcy cases of endogenously interrelated treatment and curative variables of wellbeing against the contrary case of exogenous, thereby mutative relationship between the variables of the dis-wellbeing function. Example of the first kind is complementarities between scientific mechanism of pandemic cure and arresting deepening poverty by moral consciousness in policy instrumentation. Example of the second case is inducing racial frontline nursing care to address number of afflictions of coronavirus. This practice reflects an immoral attitude of the use of human service for a wrong purpose:

> Doctors, nurses and healthcare workers are literally risking their lives on the frontline with limited resources and yet some people feel the need to impose more hatred and fear.[29]

In the case of the multidisciplinary idea with differentiated socio-scientific fields addressing the pandemic episode there is no episteme of unity of knowledge to address the science-economy-society moral inclusiveness. The utilitarian conception of welfare instead of wellbeing is now used for explaining optimal use of the representation of the welfare function. The result of such optimality yields

Welfare function, $W(x_1, x_2, \ldots, x_n)$, whereby,   (5.12)
$dW/dx_j = 0 = \Sigma_i(\partial W/\partial x_i)*(dx_i/dx_j)$,

wherein, dx_i/dx_j are negative or positive according to whether the relationship between the (x_i, x_j)-variables, $(i, j) = 1, 2, \ldots, n$ are substitutes or complements, respectively. There is no θ-effect. Marginal substitution according to neoclassical utility theory must necessarily exist, conveying methodological individualism, and thereby an extended meaning of mutation at large.

Generalization

The non-linear character of the evolutionary learning model as of the pandemic ensemble to unify the multidisciplinary field of moral inclusiveness, as described earlier, has properties and formalism that are purely of mathematical nature. The emergent IIE-model of learning in participative organism of unity of knowledge as the episteme, thereby applies universally and uniquely to all the issues and problems intra- and inter-systems in the study of pandemic episode. This means that diversity of disciplines can be studied uniquely by the same evolutionary learning formalism with the epistemic unity of knowledge in 'everything,' despite the variation in the emergent problems of diverse but knowledge-embedded systems.

The result is a unique one besides being universal by virtue of its purely mathematical nature extending to 'everything' in the sense of evolutionary learning across intra- and inter-systems. Methodological uniqueness is explained by virtue of its global nature of participative complementarities between variables, their topological transformations, and the underlying agencies being represented by the variables and relations that overarch the multidisciplinary domain of socio-scientific ensembles.

This result is contrary to the postulate of resource scarcity, opportunity cost of resource allocation, and marginal rate of substitution between competing alternatives in mainstream socio-scientific theory. A strong example of the participative case is the knowledge-induced treatment of appropriate complementarities between growth rate and poverty reduction rate. Indeed, like COVID-19, poverty is a ravaging human pandemic.

There is no endogenous (learning) theory and process model of the kind of unity of complementary interrelations to be found in the case of the pandemic regimes of control by the model of unified multidisciplinary ensemble of moral inclusiveness. In the natural sciences too, the endogenous meaning of Ghaia remains an epistemological aspiration (Primavesi, 2000).[30] In theoretical physics the words of Hawking (1988, p. 33)[31] in respect of reverse (recursive) causality is worth noting to put in place a cosmological meaning of uniqueness of methods in our moral inclusiveness model: "Space and time not only affect but also are affected by everything that happens in the universe." Social and biological Darwinism is disposed of with the logical consequence of pervasive complementarities (Xuemou & Dinghe, 1999).[32]

Towards empirical illustration of non-linear complexity in circular causation relations in the pandemic treatment and curative model

The importance of representing changes in the socio-economic variables caused by knowledge-induced variables and the knowledge-flows is a concept quite different from the trends in time-dependent observations of socio-economic variables. We have taken here the comparative trends in the growth rate of real GDP and the poverty rate as proportion of the poor in the total population. We take the example of Indonesia. These variables are induced by the ranked knowledge-values responding to degrees of complementary interrelations caused by the ranked knowledge-induced socio-scientific variables.

The important matter to note is that in the circular causation case between poverty rate, growth rate of real GDP, and the ranked knowledge-values by averaging over complementarities in the two variables, the expressions for the variables are given as follows:

$G(\theta, P(\theta); t)$ denotes the growth rate of real GDP in terms of the endogenously related poverty variable $P(\theta)$. Both variables are induced by θ-ranked values.

Likewise, $P(\theta)$ is specified.

These transforms are like the $F(f)$-functional transformations shown earlier in respect of explaining functional non-linearity caused by systemic embedding in multidimensional ensembles.

In the sheer time-dependent case of specifying these variables the relevant diagrams show the comparative time-trends of $G = G(t)$; $P = P(t)$.

Conclusion

The search for a unified theory of nature is alive not only in the natural sciences. The grand unified theory of 'everything' ought to encompass the social sciences as well. The result then would be a purposive and meaningful construction of the science-economy-society model of moral inclusiveness as a multidisciplinary knowledge-embedded interrelationship between vectors of variables representing intra- and inter-systems domains. The result then will be a unified theory of inter-causality between 'everything.' Now in the social sciences there arises the structure of a morally embedded political economy by systemic knowledge-induced embedding (Sztompka, 1974).[33] This is the concluding nature and message of the generalized model of science-economy-society moral inclusiveness. Such an ensemble model applies to all verities that complement by knowledge-flows in the framework of unity of knowledge. An example of normalization is of the pandemic mutational disorder being transformed to normalcy of cells.

This entire work has been a pointer in the previously mentioned direction of restoring cellular mutation by normalization of healthy cells. The framework of the methodological approach is universally and uniquely premised in the episteme of unity of knowledge in 'everything.' Economy shares this interactive unity richly by its immanent new theory of moral political economy and the endogeneity of ethics and economics in modelling moral inclusiveness. Sociology shares it by a new theory of the ecological and human world-system. Mathematics shares it by its emergent theory of complexity, systems, and cybernetics. Philosophy of science shares it by its demand for a new epistemological outlook of being and becoming (Thayer-Bacon, 2003).[34] The formalism introduced in this chapter thereby breaks new grounds of novelty for further investigation in mathematical socio-scientific field of intellection that includes importantly the multidisciplinary ensemble between science, economics, and social sciences in the widest model of moral inclusiveness.

Notes

1 Choudhury, M.A., Mariyanti, T. & Hossain, M.S. (2014). "A quantitative application of circular causation method in evaluating Tawhidi wellbeing and sustainable development", in Chapter Nine, Choudhury, M.A., ed. *Tawhidi Epistemology and its Applications: Economics, Finance, Science, and Society*, pp. 280–289, Cambridge Scholars Publishing, Newcastle upon Tyne, UK.
2 Hayek, F.A. (1945). "The use of knowledge in society", *American Economic Review*, 35:5, pp. 519–530.
3 Myrdal, G. (1958). "The principle of cumulation", in P. Streeten, ed. *Value in Social Theory, a Selection of Essays on Methodology by Gunnar Myrdal*, pp. 198–205, Harper & Brothers Publishers, New York, NY.
4 Beed, C. & Kane, O. (1991). "What is the critique of the mathematization of economics?", *Kyklos*, 44:4.
5 Soros, G. (1998). "Fallibility and reflexivity", in *The Crisis of Global Capitalism*, pp. 3–45, Public Affairs, New York.
6 Boland, L.A. (1991). "On the methodology of economic model building", in his *The Methodology of Economic Model Building*, pp. 39–63, Routledge, London.
7 Popper, K. (1998). *Conjectures and Refutations: The Growth of Scientific Knowledge*, Routledge & Kegan Paul, London.
8 Barrow, J.D. (1991). *Theories of Everything, the Quest for Ultimate Explanation*, Oxford University Press, Oxford.
9 George, H. (1897). *The Science of Political Economy*, Robert Schalkenbach Foundation, New York.
10 Sztompka, P. (1991). *Society in Action, The Theory of Social Becoming*, The University of Chicago Press, Chicago, IL.
11 Choudhury, M.A. (2007). *The Universal Paradigm and the Islamic World-System: Economics, Ethics, Science and Society*, World Scientific Publishers, Singapore.
12 Prigogine, I. (1980). *From Being to Becoming*, W.H. Freeman, San Francisco, CA.
13 Whitehead, A.N. (1978). *Process and Reality*, D.R. Griffin & D.W. Sherburne, eds. pp. 7, 24, 41–42, The Free Press, New York.
14 Hubner, K., trans., Dixon, P.R. Jr. & Dixon, H.M. (1985). "Foundations of a universal historistic theory of the empirical sciences", in his *Critique of Scientific Reason*, pp. 105–122, The University of Chicago Press, Chicago, IL.
15 Choudhury, M.A. (2009). "Which comes first? – knowledge or time", *Philosophical Papers and Review*, 1:4.
16 Choudhury, M.A. & Hossain, M.S. (2007). *Computing Reality*, Aoishima Research Institute, Tokyo, Japan.
17 Bertuglia, C.S. & Vaio, F. (2005). "Dynamical systems and the phase space", in *Nonlinearity, Chaos & Complexity, the Dynamics of Natural and Social Systems*, pp. 49–70, Oxford University Press, Oxford.
18 Kupka, I.A.K. & Peixoto, M.M. (1993). "On the enumerative geometry of geodesics", in M.W. Hirsch, J.E. Marsden & M. Shub, eds. *From Topology to Computation: Proceedings of the Smalefest*, pp. 243–253, Springer-Verlag, New York, NY.

19 Chichilnisky, G. (1990). "Topology and economics: The contribution of Stephen Smale", in M.W. Hirsch, J.E. Marsden & M. Shub, eds. *From Topology to Computation: Proceedings of the Smalefest*, pp. 147–161, Springer-Verlag, New York, NY.
20 Gel'fand, I.M. & Shenitzer, A. (1961). "Introduction to tensors", in their *Lectures on Linear Algebra*, pp. 164–185, Interscience Publishers, Inc., New York, NY.
21 Debreu, G. (1990). "Stephen Smale and the economic theory of general equilibrium", in M.W. Hirsch, J.E. Marsden & M. Shub, eds. *From Topology to Computation: Proceedings of the Smalefest*, pp. 131–146, Springer-Verlag, New York, NY.
22 Smale, S. (1990). "The story of the higher dimensional Poincaré conjecture (what actually) happened on the beaches of Rio)", *Mathematical Intelligence*, 12:2, pp. 44–51.
23 Myrdal, G. (1958). "The principle of cumulation", in P. Streeten, ed. *Value in Social Theory, a Selection of Essays on Methodology by Gunnar Myrdal*, pp. 198–205, Harper & Brothers Publishers, New York, NY.
24 Fitzpatrick, T. (2003). "Postmodernism and new directions", in P. Alcock, A. Erskine & M. May, eds. *The Student's Companion to Social Policy*, pp. 127–136, Blackwell Publishing, Oxford.
    Wallerstein, I. (1998). "Spacetime as the basis of knowledge", in O.F. Bordo, ed. *People's Participation, Challenges Ahead*, pp. 43–62, Apex Press, New York, NY.
25 Grandmont, J.-M. (1989). "Temporary equilibrium", in J. Eatwell, M. Milgate & P. Newman, eds. *New Palgrave: General Equilibrium*, W.W. Norton, New York, NY.
    Burstein, M. (1991). "History versus equilibrium: Joan Robinson and time in economics", in I.H. Rima, ed. *The Joan Robinson Legacy*, pp. 49–61, M.E. Sharpe, Inc, Armonk, New York.
26 Friedman, A. (1982). *Foundations of Modern Analysis*, Dover Publications, Inc.
27 Maddox, I.J. (1970). *Elements of Functional Analysis*, Cambridge University Press, Cambridge.
28 In respect of the pervasively probabilistic nature of events in the universe Hawking and Mlodinow (2010, p. 72) write: "According to quantum physics, no matter how much information we obtain or how powerful our computing abilities, the outcomes of physical processes cannot be predicted with certainty because they are not determined with certainty." Hawking, S.W. & Mlodinow, L. (2010). *The Grand Design*, Bantam Books, New York, NY.
29 Such a multilinear relationship of evolutionary nonlinear functionals can be represented as a mathematical tensor functional (Gel'fand & Shenitzer, 1961, op cit). The following is the way to write tensor functionals: $(\mathbf{x(\theta),f(x(\theta));(Fof)(x(\theta)))} = a_{ij}k.\xi^i\eta^j\zeta_k$, where, $\mathbf{x(\theta)} = \xi^i.e_i$; $\mathbf{f(x(\theta))} = \eta^j.e_j$; $\mathbf{(Fof)(x(\theta))} = \zeta k.ek$. (ei; ej) are the contravariant basis vectors of region R. e^k are the covariant basis vectors of $\mathbf{(Fof)(x(\theta))}$ in region R^, which is the dual of covariant vector space of region R, meaning the functionals that are linearly additive of nonlinear functionals in R.
30 Gilroy, R. (March 20, 2020). "Nurses on coronavirus frontline facing 'abhorrent' abuse from public", *Nursing Times*.
31 Primavesi, A. (2000). *Sacred Gaia*, Routledge, London.
32 Hawking, S.W. (1988). "Space and time", in his *Brief History of Time*, Bantam Books, New York, NY.
33 Xuemou, W. & Dinghe, G. (1999). "Pansystems cybernetics, framework, methodology and development", *Kybernetes, International Journal of Systems and Cybernetics*, 28:6&7, pp. 679–694.
34 Sztompka, P. (1974). "Systemic models in functional analysis", in *System and Function, Towards a Theory of Society*, pp. 47–57, Academic Press, New York, NY.

6 The role of educational reform in COVID-19 normalization

Background

In the discussion between Rob Johnson, the director of the Institute for New Economic Thinking (INET, July 2020), and Professor Michael Sandel, Harvard Political Philosopher, we heard about the following deepening concern from Sandel:

> Since this pandemic began, we've heard a slogan. We're all in this together. That's a slogan of solidarity. We hear it from politicians, from advertisers, from celebrities. And that slogan to me doesn't so much describe a fact or a condition. It poses a question. Are we really all in this together? Or does the pandemic reveal the effect that decades of widening inequality have had on our common life?

Furthermore, Sandel expressed his concern on the much-needed extensive democratization of universal participation by all echelons of global and national society at large. His words are (edited):

> So I think if there's to be a source of hope, not to say salvation, but at least of democratic hope, it lies less with markets and with government; and more with revitalizing civil society, and renewing democratic public discourse, and broadening its reach. So that we can engage with neighbors, with the fellow workers. But also, with the national community. And ideally engage with those across national boundaries. So, the institutions of civil society, the forms of civic engagement that can take place there. Together with a broadened, more morally engaged kind of public discourse. These I see as a source of hope. For democratic renewal, more than trying to design institutions of a global governance on the one hand or casting our fate to markets on the other. That seems

to me that only the best source of hope, Rob. I don't know whether, do you see it that way? Or how do you view it?

(Sandel, The Tyranny of Merit: What's Become of
the Common Good? September 2020).[1]

The backbone of change that existed before the COVID-19 episode and deepened thereafter, and yet cannot be seen to embrace a subtle wind of change is the existing unacceptable continuity in the elitist nature of educational program as a critical aftermath to discuss following COVID-19 pandemic times. This accumulating problem of scientific, economic, and social differentiation is neither felt nor pronounced at all levels of educational programs with the air of conscious reformation and future concern. The concerns lie on all of the underlying predicaments of the ultimate causes of generalized pandemic episodes. The resulting causes of such pandemic are many. Among these are Covid-19, human poverty, social inequality in wealth and opportunities, and resource distribution for participatory ownership widely across the social and economic order (Shakespeare, 1999).[2] These are issues that existed since time immemorial and received continued affirmation over time. They assumed unbroken garb under different forms of global authoritarianism. Among these excruciating human experiences are those imposed by feudalism (Holton, op. cit.); capitalism (Pickety, op. cit.); and liberalism and socialism (Hayek, 1967).[3]

On the eve of a Global Forum on Socio-Scientific Issues of COVID-19 Episode organized by me with our learned group, Professor Robert D. Crane, Professor Emeritus of Islamic Studies, Qatar University, wrote on the historical and the present much-needed reversion to *Jus Divinum*. In Islam this is qur'anic monotheism as divine law of oneness expressed in terms of unity of knowledge of the human race in a unified world-system of wellbeing and purpose. He wrote:

The current moment in modern civilization, triggered in part by the unprecedented COVID-19 pandemic, opens opportunities for self-examination. This may be particularly true for the diverse peoples in the United States of America, who have begun to fear even for their personal existence and increasingly distrust and even fear the status quo based on elitist leadership through economic oligarchy and a growing wealth gap at home and through inevitable failures in both economic and military dominance abroad.

The opportunities are opening for the pursuit of "compassionate justice" as the essence of leadership in a leaderless world.

This, in turn, creates opportunities for leaders in all of the world religions, including the indigenous, to define the essence, principles, and application of compassionate justice. This is the task, respectively, of ontology, epistemology, and axiology though peaceful engagement from the bottom up in a pluralist world.

The ontological principles in Islamic thought can be reduced to the following four principles of guidance:

1) *Haqq al din*: freedom of religion based on respect for the common identity in the essence of all world religions.
2) *Haqq al nafs:* Respect for the sacredness of the individual person deriving from God.
3) *Haqq al nasl*: Respect for human community, including organic nations based on common heritage, common values in the present, and common hopes for the future.
4) *Haqq al mahid* (from *wahid*, one, *wahda*, oneness): Respect for the physical environment, including the understanding that land does not belong to us, but we belong to the land.

These four epistemological requirements for compassionate justice are all interdependent. No single one can be adequately respected without the others, just as all of these epistemological requirements are dependent on all of the ontological principles.

The requirements for compassionate justice are the courses of action necessary to respect the transcendent ontological guidelines and the related principles for action in an environment of different and changing contexts.

Educational reform to discover pandemic renormalization

The age-old philosophy of education has always proceeded along self-conceited outlook of elitism and a socio-economic development context of economic growth and acquisition of wealth and property rights. The prominent impression of such a pursuit of educational programs has always been devoid of any programmatic and policy-centered incentive for understanding the greater issues and problems of the global society and its economic reasoning and structure with the science-economy-society moral inclusiveness. As an example, it has been pronounced that educational programs feed into models of cash-flows, economic growth, efficiency, self-centered property rights, and human resource development. The misunderstood idea of such achievements is garlanded on education as having its trickle-down effects on economy, finance, science, and society. These elitist consequences have altogether decried the great moral inclusiveness issues that a holistic model of education and educational reform ought to cultivate human and environmental wellbeing.

A serious actionable criticism leading to educational reformation for attaining the wellbeing objective criterion could not be realized. Thereby, the objective of a participatory worldview – contrary to the self-centered goals of human resource development, human capital investment, acquisitive future of output, income, growth, self-interest, and the ignorance of restructuring economy and society towards seriously realizing poverty alleviation and the like – could not be realized.

These forgotten despairing points of the nature, study, and policy directions of human capital theory (Becker, 1994; Schultz, 1971)[4] have caused this field of scientific economic study to be entrenched in neoclassical economic reasoning of competing for scarce resources and upholding the belief on marginal rate of substitution between economic and socio-moral sides of educational reformation in their opposite sides. Consequently, Banerjee and Duflo (op. cit.) point out regarding the continuing global pandemic of povertythat the neoclassical aspect of educational and human resource deepening practice in favour of the trickle-down claim of human capital theory and marginalization of the moral focus of education in science-economy-society interrelationship at large continue to prevail. Banerjee and Duflo write:

> What does it matter whether regulations conserve human resources if there is barrier to their entry by the poor?
>
> Human resource development by public policy does not reach the benefits for the very poor. All forms of human resources apply here: education of the type used in human capital investment; water resources, land as resource, technology as resource; health as resource.
>
> The indicator of increase in consumption per capita seen as being congenial for economic growth does mean much for the very poor. The menu of the very poor is not highlighted in consumption.

In regard to the poor effectiveness of elitist education on the children of the poor the authors write:

> *Poor Economics* is ultimately about what the lives and choices of the poor tell us about how to fight global poverty. It helps us to understand, for example, why microfinance is useful without being the miracle some hoped it would be; why the poor often end up with health care that does them more harm than good; why children of the poor can go to school year after year and not learn anything; why the poor don't want

health insurance; and it reveals why so many magic bullets of yesterday have ended up as today's failed ideas.

Economics and business programs are now faced up against the need for tremendous conceptual and applied changes. These changes are necessary to liberate the scientific, economic, and social fields from their neoclassical outlook and social Darwinism. Instead then it is necessary during the pandemic times to formalize the model of science-economy-society moral inclusiveness. This is a pressing educational and global policy directive of the time. That is educational policies in the neoclassical mold have failed, even as the existing curriculums have fallen decrepit in addressing human issues of wellbeing and the issues of moral sustainability of the common good. Such human objective goals are apart from what they are presently. That is a utilitarian self-interested maximizing calculus of pain and pleasure, welfare, and social choices of philosophizing the notion of human capital revolution without the moral focus (Gintis & Bowles, 1975).[5]

Now with alarming pandemic of many types, continuing economic uncertainty, global poverty, inequality, and deprivation of opportunities, the words of Banerjee and Duflo shore on the human landscape:

> Globally, more than 700 million people live in extreme poverty, according to the World Bank, which defines poverty as living on less than $1.90 per day. One in three children is malnourished, according to figures provided by the Nobel Foundation, and most children leave school without basic skills in reading, writing, and math.

The neoclassical origin of disempowerment prevails at all levels. Its global ravages start from the entire rung of educational programs, educational policies, and the labor market and economic and business fronts. Educational programs and philosophy as they exist today in a disempowered world-system has been entrenched in the economic and social order as an accepted culture and norm. This state of the neoclassical elitist mind must change into an educational reformation of science-economy-society model of moral inclusiveness. Thereby, the educational programs must reform along with their curriculum design; modes of teaching and delivery with eclectic focus; and innovative and substantive conceptual and applied methods. Such affective changes ought to frame the policy directives and global institutional emphasis in tune with the changes in accordance with the labor market and economic and business possibilities. The pandemic of poverty along with those enigmas that cause poverty, as the case of present COVID-19 episode and the elitist world-system, must be engaged in the echelons of educational rendering with the force of human ecological goodness (Hawley, op. cit.).

The higher echelons of educational programs for socio-economic development, such as the UNDP, OECD, World Bank, UNESCO, and leading consortiums of universities around the world must all take upon them the educational transformation task seriously. Consequently, there is to be a profound analytical model of science-economy-society moral inclusiveness to engage the underlying multidisciplinary holism of the ensuing conceptual and applied educational outlook along with the coterminous science-economy-society moral inclusiveness.

All this does not mean reducing the scientific rigor of the educational good. The educational transformation must be objectively oriented for wellbeing and equality of opportunities and capabilities for all. This totality of mankind must comprise those in the ignored 'basti' (slums) and its interactive learning and participatory human part comprising the conscious part of the thoughtful. The two human parts will learn and teach mutually the multidisciplinary perspective of education and skills by the moral episteme, philosophy, and conscious practice. The resulting model of science-economy-society moral inclusiveness will abide by the moral will and policy-theoretic enforcement in respect of global wellbeing and the common good.

Figure 6.1 explains the opposing nature of the two kinds of changes – between the neoclassical and the wellbeing model of unity of knowledge in moral inclusiveness. Also explained here is the internal properties of these distinct models in the context of methodological individualism and its inability to formalize the model of multidisciplinary ensemble in the neoclassical case. In the case of the wellbeing model of multidisciplinary complementarity by the episteme of unity of knowledge the issue of moral inclusiveness is answered, practiced, and abides in sustainability.

In reference to Figure 6.1, in neoclassical socio-economics the abiding property of methodological individualism implies $\cap_i\{x_i'\} = \phi$. That is $\{x_i'\}$ are statistically independent. Thereby, the functional transformation holds by $\cup_i\cap_i\{f_i'(x_i')\}=\Sigma_i f_i'(x_i')$. Likewise, $\cup_i[\{f_i'(x_i')\} \cap_i \{f_i(x_i(\theta))\}] = \cup_i\{\phi_i\} = \phi$. This also implies $\{\Sigma[\{f_i'(x_i')\}\cup\{f_j(x_j(\theta))\}] = \phi$. This result implies linearity of disjoint relationship between two types of functions, $\{f_i'(x_i')\},\{f_j(x_j(\theta))\}$.

In the θ-knowledge-induced formalism of science-economy-society moral inclusiveness, the form of $\{f_j(x_j(\theta))\}$ is non-linear and complex in the wellbeing objective criterion with endogenous inter-variable circular causation equations and the quantitative evaluative form of the wellbeing function. Thereby, $\cap^{integration}_j\{x_j(\theta)\} \neq \phi$; $\cup^{interaction}_j\cap^{integration}_j\{f_j(x_j(\theta))\}\neq \phi \neq \Sigma_j f_j(x_j(\theta))$ as linear functions that would imply methodological individualism between the linearly independent variables and their systems. Lastly, $(d/d\theta)[\cup^{interaction}_j\cap^{integration}_j\{f_j(x_j(\theta))\}] > 0$. The specific case of $f_j(x_j(\theta)$ is the

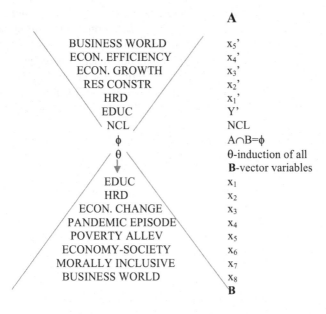

Figure 6.1 Contrasting knowledge-induced parametric model and the neoclassical economic approach in the structure of pandemic treatment and renormalization

system-specific wellbeing function. The specifics are generalized in pandemic episodes such as of COVID-19, poverty, business and economic uncertainty, global unemployment, and the like in the grand scale.

Differentiating socio-economic growth and endogenous ethical development between neoclassical and knowledge-induced models of pandemic episodes

It is well known and has been stated in this work that neoclassical economic growth by its ceteris paribus method of calculating the optimum goals ignores the ethical factors as being endowed by endogenous functional effects. Economic growth models limit their studies to relations between output and its rate of change in relation to the variable factors of capital and labor, savings and investment, technology, population change, and capital depreciation rate (Solow, 1980).[6] In the closest endogenous form of growth model (Romer, 1986)[7] together with Solow's neoclassical growth model the pandemic episode of poverty, famine, and deprivation consequences that neoclassicism attributes to population growth remain unexplained.

According to Solow's economic growth model of constant resource to scale the per capita real growth model is written as y = K/L. Contrarily, in the θ-induced endogenous growth model the formalism is different from Romer's growth model. With the θ-induction the increasing returns to scale, denoted by n, per capita real production function is given by $y^n(\theta) = f(K(\theta)/L(\theta)) = f(k(\theta))$. The increasing returns to scale implies the positive q-effect of endogenous resource increase on $f(k(\theta))$. Thereby the presence of marginal productivity of $k(\theta)$ is annulled. This is contrary to the neo-classical marginal productivity principle of y = f(k) in Solow's economic growth model. In this case the pandemic episodes negatively affect output as the case would be because of the marginal rate of substitution between pandemic incidence and economic activity.

Only the disabling effects of such factors on human wellbeing and the environment are studied exogenously outside science-economy-society moral attention. The emergent studies in these fields thereby remain disjoint understanding of science-economy-society models without the study of moral inclusiveness. No methodology and analytical method exist in socio-scientific methodology to integrate the diverse systemic elements in a comprehensive holistic model of moral inclusiveness. The ultimate structure of interactively integrated and evolutionary learning models of pandemic treatment and normalization take the generalized form of the wellbeing objective criterion that is evaluated (statistically estimated and simulated) across interactive, integrative, and evolutionary (IIE) learning processes. The resulting inter-variable circular causation relations and the quantitative wellbeing function in the endogenously interrelated knowledge-induced variables altogether form the multi-systemic IIE-model of moral inclusiveness for the study of pandemic treatment and normalization.

The structure of the previously mentioned type of IIE-model is explained by the underlying analytics of expression (6.1). This model is one of a large family of pandemic normalization models that can be formalized. The two-directional arrows imply endogenous inter-variable circular causal relations between critical variables that must complement together in normalizing generalized forms of pandemic episodes. The ultimate objective criterion of wellbeing is symbolized next by the circular IIE-learning processes towards treatment and cure, as viruses learn to normalize by impact of learnt treatments.

In Figure 6.2, separate categories of variables, such as {moral ensemble}, {imponderables}, {socio-economic variables}, and {medical variables} can be evaluated by their own wellbeing functions in respect of their structural equations of circular causation relations and modes of collecting data between secondary sources (published) and primary sources (questionnaire survey). Such a method of wellbeing evaluation by compounding of the system-wise wellbeing functions was mentioned in an earlier chapter.

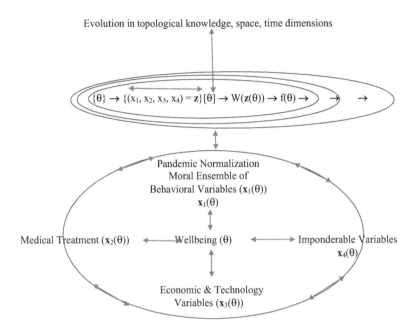

Evolution in topological knowledge, space, time dimensions

$$\{\theta\} \rightarrow \{(x_1, x_2, x_3, x_4) = z\}[\theta] \rightarrow W(z(\theta)) \rightarrow f(\theta) \rightarrow \quad \rightarrow \quad \rightarrow$$

Pandemic Normalization
Moral Ensemble of
Behavioral Variables ($x_1(\theta)$)
$x_1(\theta)$

Medical Treatment ($x_2(\theta)$) ←——Wellbeing (θ) ←————→ Imponderable Variables
$x_4(\theta)$

Economic & Technology
Variables ($x_3(\theta)$)

Figure 6.2 Endogenous interrelations between critical wellbeing variables in normalizing pandemic episodes

Here we argue against other analytical results of neoclassical economic theory and application that contradict the possibility of using these results for attaining normalization of pandemic conditions. Of especial cases are COVID-19 and the incidence of poverty as global socio-economic pandemic episodes. Here is the better of Solow's neoclassical growth model that may be examined under endogenous growth theory, yet without the endogenous ethical effect in the details of economy-society modelling of pandemic treatment, normalization, and cure. We enquire further whether greater details of the pandemic episode can be modelled for deeper deconstruction of pandemic causes of such episodes.

Neoclassical economic growth model and endogenous economic growth model cannot explain the causes of poverty on economic growth

Let the endogenous growth (Y) model (Romer, 1986)[8] be defined by

$$Y = F(x_1, x_2, x_3, x_4) \tag{6.1}$$

Despite the interrelations between these variables, as for instance between moral ensemble variables and economic variables, no transmigration effect is recognized between the moral value of organized charity towards stemming the incidence of poverty by way of reforming the economic self-interest. For instance Friedman (1992)[9] believed that the only ethical function of the market order is profit-maximization. According to Friedman, "The doctrine of 'social responsibility', that corporations should care about the community and not just profit, is highly subversive to the capitalist system and can only lead towards totalitarianism" (in Friedman, M. *Capitalism & Freedom* op cit. https://en.wikipedia.org/ wiki/Capitalism_and_Freedom).

Likewise, while there is endogenous relationship between medical science and economy/technology, there does not exist any endogenous relationship between imponderable variables and medical science variables. Thereby, by the continuity of inter-causal relations there does not exist endogenous relations between imponderable variables, medical science variables, and economic variables. Establishing such continuity between the various multidisciplinary domains would necessitate inter-cultural understanding, adequate funding for participatory practices between modern medicine and alternative medicine, and increasing coherence in scientific terminologies of various practices to be adopted commonly.

Important imponderable values that enable the afflicted ones to remain peacefully strong manifest the divine power of prayer, coexisting environment, civic neighbourhood, community, cleanliness, and ethical attitudes. These values are assumed in neoclassical economic theory and in existing socio-scientific theories not to have any productive consequences in science, economy, technology, and modernity. The result is the missing empowerment of self-reliance in values. Within such imponderable values and by means of them the total meaning of socio-economic development can be conveyed to the alleviation of pandemic poverty and its depriving causes and effects.

The South Commission (p. 13)[10] defines the full meaning of development as follows: "To sum up: development is a process of self-reliant growth, achieved through participation of the people acting in their own interests as they see them, and under their own control." In accordance with this holistic and evolutionary learning nature of socio-economic development by endogeneity between all the variables shown in Figure 6.2, the expression (6.2) must hold. Yet it is not possible in either the neoclassical economic school or the endogenous growth theory's inability to establish sustainability by continuity of the circular causation shown in Figure 6.2.

The growth rate g_y as,

$$g_y = \Sigma_{i=1}^{4} MP_{xi}*g_{xi} \tag{6.2}$$

is undefined in the absence of definitions of growth rates of x_1 and x_4 and of the marginal productivities (MP) of these variables. Thereby, if we take x_1 to represent the vector of several poverty alleviation variables, and this vector being undefined, none of the causes of the poverty pandemic is identifiable in the growth model. No quantitative policy implication on pandemic poverty alleviation can therefore be derived.

If now COVID-19 is a source of deepening poverty in the afflicted developing world, then depressive economic growth rate cannot be justifiably attributed to the adversely affected MP measures of the poor as it is responsible on the MP_{x2}, MP_{x3}, g_{x2} and g_{x3} and their measured components. Therefore, economic growth rate g_y as measured by x_2 and x_3 in expression (6.2) is inappropriately defined by this expression.

The data in the next tables in fact show that the structure of the economy ought to change to agri-based industries in the short run. The global real economic growth rate turndown is found not to be adversely affected by real value-added of the agri-based sector. Whereas the increase in the population of the poor by additional poor joining this group is causing the adverse economic growth. The inference to be gathered from this trend is that the international economic order requires restructuring the economy

Table 6.1 COVID-19 global economic recession in 2020 (April 2020 IFPRI Global Reference Scenario)

	Percentage Change from Base Year Values				
	Real GDP	*Household consumption*	*Export of goods (value in constant dollars)*	*Agrifood Real Value Added*	*Agrifood exports (value in constant dollars)*
World	−5.0	−1.0	−20.9	−1.8	−24.8
Developed countries	−6.2	−0.1	−23.5	−3.1	−23.8
Developing countries	−3.6	−2.5	−18.0	+0.1	−30.5
Africa South of Sahara	−8.9	−3.2	−35.2	+3.9	−20.6
South Asia	−5.0	−3.7	−27.1	−2.0	−30.7
South-East Asia	−7.0	−4.2	−27.7	−2.8	−31.9
Latin America	−5.9	−4.4	−30.8	−3.9	−28.5

Source: Laborde, D. Martin, W., & Vos, R., (16 April 2020). "Poverty and food insecurity could grow dramatically as COVID-19 spreads." *Research Post.*

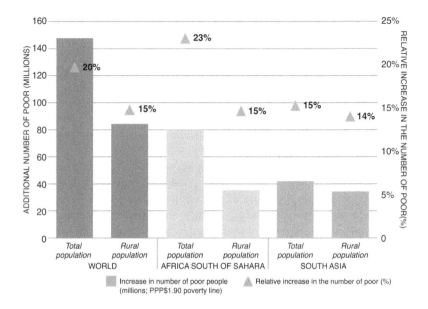

Figure 6.3 Impact of COVID-19 global economic crisis on extreme poverty

Source: Laborde, D. Martin, W., & Vos, R., (16 April 2020). "Poverty and food insecurity could grow dramatically as COVID-19 spreads." *Research Post.*

into rural transformation. As it stands the slowdown in economic growth is shown to be caused by the adversity of the industrial sector that is heaving on global poverty. The responsibility on economic structural change rests on the industrial sector for the onslaught of COVID-19 on poverty.

The inner causes of the pandemic of poverty, whose one cause is COVID-19 in most recent times, remain unexplained in the neoclassical and endogenous growth theory kinds of the economic growth models. The variables like x_1 and x_4 cannot thereby be explained by their inner components of the causes of economic growth as in its usual formulation that contradict the inappropriately explained role of economic growth relating to the wellbeing of the poor.

The 'incapability' of the poor

A theory of 'incapability' of the global poor as a case of pandemic episode and that which is critically related with COVID-19 in the reign of social inequality and development disarray can be framed in relation to the foregoing facts of economic growth. The COVID-19 cause of unemployment in Bangladesh garments factories is one example of a shameful case of young women unemployment. They comprise over a million, a 25% unemployment rate, caused by international brand fashioners abandoning to renew contracts with Bangladeshi garments companies and these stopping to pay wages of garment factory workers. The fact of this social predicament of mammoth unemployment here points to the fact that it is the industrial sector at home and the principal contracting mega-corporations abroad that bear the responsibility of high unemployment even of low-wage earners without reprieve. The relatively better facts regarding agri-based economic activity globally points out the option of the wiser alternative to remain active in the Bangladeshi abundant agricultural sector. The disabling break of the agri-based industry from the industrial sector, particularly garments, has weighed heavily upon Bangladesh during COVID-19 in regard to the garments sector. And this is just one of the many pandemic ravages on Bangladesh in particular and the industrial sector globally in general.

Such industrial calamities are of yet another form of pandemic episode on the poor. They are causing, and the development in Bangladesh is being further disabled, by abject poverty, unemployment, hunger, and misery caused by continuous natural calamities. Structural economic change with diverse sectoral complementarities in economic activities is essential to mitigate Bangladesh dismay of economy-society disempowerment. These kinds of calamities in Bangladesh as an example of a country that has abandoned her agri-based activities for greater emphasis on industrial development are no less than viral mutations of Bangladesh economy in widespread socio-economic adversities. Such an industrial episode has effects that pervade, as is the case in the wake of coronavirus episode and it's like?

Professor Amartya Sen[11] (1999, 1986) has formulated his capability, commodities, functioning, and wellbeing interrelated theory centered on his focus upon human development, poverty alleviation, and balanced development paradigm. Likewise, our 'incapability theory' of pandemic episode of socio-economic development states that in Sen's sequencing of wellbeing, the absence of any of the loops of the 'capability' chain will dismember the entire development consequences taken up in the minutest details. There is no automatic recovery of the broken chain except to point out by evaluation of the wellbeing function criterion where in the chain the disruption takes place and its depth and cause occur so that reconstruction can take place. This latter correction of the incapability case is done by simulation of the circular causation equations in quantifying the wellbeing function.

Figure 6.2 when adapted to Sen and Nussbaum's[12] (Stanford Encyclopedia of Philosophy, 2011)[13] entire theory of capability and wellbeing would yield the following socio-economic development outlook:

$$(\mathbf{x}_1, \mathbf{x}_4) = \mathbf{z}_1 \ (\mathbf{x}_2, \mathbf{x}_3) = \mathbf{z}_2 \qquad\qquad (6.3)$$

$(\mathbf{x}_{11}, \mathbf{x}_{12}, ..\mathbf{x}_{1n1}; \mathbf{x}_{41}, \mathbf{x}_{42}, ... \mathbf{x}_{4n4})$ $(\mathbf{x}_{21}, \mathbf{x}_{22}, ..\mathbf{x}_{2n2}; \mathbf{x}_{31}, \mathbf{x}_{32}, ... \mathbf{x}_{3n3})$
Further vector components   Further vector components
Capabilities: Imponderables   Commodities, Functioning: Materiality
Disjointness: $\{\mathbf{z}_1\}\cap\{\mathbf{z}_2\} = \phi$ in the neoclassical ceteris paribus view.
$$\downarrow$$
Wellbeing function
$$W(\mathbf{z}_1, \mathbf{z}_2, \mathbf{z}_3, \mathbf{z}_4)$$

$W(\mathbf{z})$ may exist as defined in respect of utilitarian concept, welfare economics, and social choice theory (Harsanyi, 1955).[14] The neoclassical property of marginal substitution can exist also within $\{\mathbf{z}_1\}$ and $\{\mathbf{z}_2\}$. $W(\mathbf{z})[\theta]$ does not exist but can be corrected by simulation under the paradigm of IIE and by unity of knowledge explained by $\{\theta\}$, subject to inter-variable circular causation relations. Contrarily, in neoclassical economic theory there does not exist endogenous circular causation relation like, $z_{1i} = f_{1i}(\mathbf{z}_{1j})$; $z_{2k} = f_{1i}(\mathbf{z}_{2s})$; $x_u = f_u(\mathbf{x}_v)$; with $(i, j) = 1(11, 12, ... 1n1), 4 (41, 42, ..., 4n4), i \neq j$. $(k,s) = 2 (21, 22, ..., 2n2), 3 (31, 32, ..., 3n3), k \neq s$. $(u,v) = 1(11, .., 1n1), 2(21, 22, .., 2n2), 3(31, 32, ..., 3n3), 4(41, 42, ..., 4n4), u \neq v$.

In conclusion to this section, our 'theory of incapability' is explained by the feature of discontinuity between the imponderable and mechanistic variables of the wellbeing function in respect of Sen's development categories of capability, functioning, commodities, and the resulting wellbeing. The distinctive feature noted beyond Sen's wellbeing categories is the especial definition that the wellbeing objective criterion acquires in reference to its ontology of unity of knowledge and that reflects its complete holistic working in the wellbeing function. This objective criterion is quantitatively evaluated along with its inter-variable circular causation relations. The meaning of evaluation here is that of estimation of the entire system of the wellbeing objective criterion and its endogenous inter-variable system of circular causation. Estimation of the coefficients of the predictor endogenous variables is next simulated to change the estimated coefficients and predictor variables in desired ways possible by policy choices and conscious institutional discourse within the science-economy-society model of moral inclusiveness.

Multidisciplinary project valuation with fullness of complementary variables

Many philanthropic and well-organized governments have for long been practicing social security, guaranteed income, and medical guarantee for low-income families. Such financial insurance for the low-income recipient citizens has paved the way towards perpetual national wellbeing. Thereby, fiscal policy of national spending on social security in its broad meaning contains in this formula financing of public funds by moral and material resource allocation. This practice is found to exist particularly in the exemplary case of Canadian social security.[15] Another is the exemplary case of the Scandinavian social security.[16]

Many corporations now include formula financing of human and environmental ethical concerns. The well-known example of this kind is corporate social responsibility (CSR). As a social term by its conveyance though, its practice is limited to spending on ethical outlets and thereby receiving tax rebate at the business level. This return in turn compensates the firm for the incurred costs of CSR. Besides, the additional production cost of the CSR goods transferred on to the consumer causes an increase in the social transaction cost of socio-ethical benefits. Prices increase thereby as the component of consumer spending. An example of this is that the rollover of social transaction cost in goods and services on the consumer defeats the role of consciousness of ethicality as internalized endogenous moral value of CSR.

An example of such a conscious internalization of social values was formalized by Choudhury (2014)[17] based on the following conception: the science-economy-society model of moral inclusiveness gives the nature of the creative firm as a cooperator rather than a competitor. Thereby, the theory of the firm in such a case is different from the profit and output maximizing objective of the neoclassical producer. The contrary firm as a participative producer and seller extends the activities of the resulting participative firm. In this case, the complementary goals of extensive moral inclusiveness make the firms as a paired institution with market, self, and other participating combinations. The kinds of firms that so emerge are learning institutions between the producer, distributor, and buyer across the private, public, and global sectors of the world-system. Our earlier studied dynamics of interaction, integration, and evolutionary learning between diverse entities, agents, and agencies of the conscious social economy is invoked.

Within such a complex of participation, all the aggregate and disaggregate variables explained in Figure 6.2 give rise to pertinent definitions and applications, teaching, and morally inclusive consciousness. The implications of economic and social ideas of production, consumption, productivity, efficiency, and wellbeing are changed in subtle ways of moral inclusiveness. The earlier explained conception of 'incapability' contrary to the 'capability' concept forms the underlying extensive science-economy-society multidisciplinary ensemble of moral inclusiveness. We refer to the emergent world-view of corporate social responsibility in concert with the complementary domain of unity of knowledge. The emergent concept of CSR is termed as conscious corporate social responsibility (CCSR) in its substantive sense of conscious invoking of moral values endogenously invoked.

Choudhury (2014 op. cit.) formalizes the objective criterion of science-economy-society with moral inclusiveness by the following approach to the emergent analytical modelling. As it was explained regarding the new features of the neoclassical economic growth model and the endogenous growth model, inter-variable complementarities and abstracto-empirical consciousness meaning of the circular causation relations must be well defined. In the imminent pervasively complementary domain of unity of knowledge, consciousness as a well-defined function of unity of knowledge by universal pairing between the good things as permissible entities and avoidance of pandemic episodes embed all conscious practices.

With all such science-economy-society moral inclusiveness in the abstracto-empirical sense of consciousness, the CCSR model of production and consumption derived from the wellbeing objective criterion is written as

$$W(Q,C,M,T,\vartheta_1,\vartheta_2)[\theta(\varepsilon)] = W_1(Q,C,M,T)[\theta(\varepsilon)]*W_2(\vartheta_1,\vartheta_2)[\theta(\varepsilon)] \quad (6.4)$$

The term abstracto-empirical means the embedding of imponderable ontological moral values in materiality of being and becoming of the diverse world-system. These moral values blended endogenously form the implicative nature of consciousness as the abstracto-empirical phenomena. Such a science-economy-society transformation in moral inclusiveness is what Michio Kaku (2015, p. 43)[18] refers to in the abstracto-materiality sense: "Consciousness is the process of creating a model of the world using multiple feedback loops in various parameters." In our case of developing a multidisciplinary moral ensemble model of pandemic control, the science-economy-society materiality and imponderables denote the various parameters. This case was also denoted in expression (6.3).

$Q(\theta(\varepsilon))$ denotes joint production function of complementary life-sustaining outputs, $Q_i(\theta(\varepsilon))$. $Q(\theta(\varepsilon))$ denotes participative sectoral production shared by joint production functions of complementary life-sustaining productions, $Q_i(\theta(\varepsilon))$. These variables form the disaggregated vector components shown in expression (6.3) to combat the 'incapability' adversities of poverty caused by pandemic situations. Thus,

$$Q(\theta(\varepsilon)) = A_0(\theta)\Pi_i Q_i^{ai}(\theta(\varepsilon)) \quad (6.5)$$

$C(\theta(\varepsilon))$ denotes community-shared joint consumption function of complementary life-sustaining goods and services, $C_j(\theta(\varepsilon))$. These elements also form the disaggregated vector components shown in expression (6.3) to combat the 'incapability' caused by poverty as yet another example of pandemic situations. Thus,

$$C(\theta(\varepsilon)) = A_1(\theta(\varepsilon))\Pi_j C_j^{bj}(\theta(\varepsilon)) \qquad (6.6)$$

$M(\theta(\varepsilon))$ denotes a compound index of various finance mobilizing instruments, $M_k(\theta(\varepsilon))$, which denote those financial instruments that enable economy-money capability, commodities, functioning, and wellbeing and deter the incidence of 'incapability' caused by poverty as an example of pandemic situation. Thus,

$$M(\theta(\varepsilon)) = A_2(\theta(\varepsilon))\Pi_k C_k^{ck}(\theta(\varepsilon)) \qquad (6.7)$$

Likewise, $T(\theta(\varepsilon))$ denotes technological change denoting the intensification of particular kinds of choice of technology by sectoral diversification and equally labor-capital augmenting technological change for enhancing participative socio-economic development across all possible complementary enabling entities. Thus,

$$T(\theta(\varepsilon)) = A_3(\theta(\varepsilon))\Pi_s C_s^{ds}(\theta(\varepsilon)) \qquad (6.8)$$
$$\text{Let, } \vartheta_1(\theta(\varepsilon)) \text{ and } \vartheta_2(\theta(\varepsilon)) \qquad (6.9)$$

denote imponderable variables based on human civic values, global neighbourhood, and the like (Commission on Global Governance, 1995),[19] and spirituality.[20] Data on these variables are acquired by questionnaire surveys. Observations so collated are converted by geometric or arithmetic averages. Data collected by survey across respondents can be collated together for $J_1(\theta(\varepsilon))$ and $J_2(\theta(\varepsilon))$.[21]

We note that all variables in their aggregate and disaggregate vectors, thereby in their microeconomic state economy-wide, are governed by IIE-learning properties of imponderable attributes that induce knowledge formation respecting a participative world-system of unity of knowledge. The correcting possibilities of pandemic control and their adverse consequences are realized uniformly across science-economy-society by the underlying multidisciplinary model of moral inclusiveness.

The compounding expression (6.4) of $W_1(..)$ and $W_2(..)$ points out how two distinct data sets, secondary and primary with different range of observations, are used to evaluate the wellbeing functions in materiality and imponderable variables of the multidisciplinary ensemble. Each of these individual wellbeing segments of the total $W(..)$ has its evaluated quantitative segments, say θ_1 and θ_2, respectively. Thereby, for the whole quantitative form of the wellbeing function, $\theta = \gamma(\theta)*\theta_1^a\theta_2^\beta$ in generalized sense with the coefficients as functions of their respective knowledge parameters.

In completeness of the objective function of wellbeing for the governance of pandemic episodes of various kinds, referred to in this chapter by poverty as cause and effect of COVID-19, the multidisciplinary model of science-economy-society moral inclusiveness is now formalized as follows:

Expression (6.4) → W(. .) = Product of expressions (6.5)-(6.9) across the respective range of subscripts, given the individual analytical treatment of W_1(. .) and W_2(. .) forms the full complementary model of wellbeing indexes of the science-economy-society-wide moral inclusiveness as explained in expression (6.3) arising from Figure 6.2.[22] In this model the attributes {ε} determine the consciousness element of every variable characterizing the system to which they belong. We refer to this consciousness as CCSR. Upon the ensuing wellbeing index W(. .) the capability of the entire model is established contrary to pandemic episodes – outburst of poverty in regard to COVID-19. The resulting wellbeing evaluation model describes the IIE-learning properties of the ontology of unity of knowledge. The endogenous nature of the full complementary model of science-economy-society moral inclusiveness being induced by {θ(e)} causes CCSR to create socio-economic structures and the extensively participated policies while reducing transaction cost in realizing such matters. The result of such endogenously emergent participatory science-economy-society moral inclusiveness is sustainability of human values in respect of the episteme of unity of knowledge. Wilson (1998)[23] referred to this state of endogenous mind-matter interrelations as consilience. Wilson writes (p. 266): "Science pushed too far is science arrogant. Let it keep its proper place, as the God-given gifts to understand His physical domain."

Time variables in the generalized model of science-economy-society-wide model of moral inclusiveness

Time and process are not the same in the IIE-learning model of unity of knowledge with its sustainability in science-economy-society moral inclusiveness. That is because the IIE-learning properties continue either intra-system or inter-system. In the intra-system case of evaluation of the wellbeing function associated with capability, commodities, and functioning the additional feature of inter-variable circular causation as shown in expression (6.3) appears in the form of estimation followed by desired appropriate simulation of the coefficients of the model. In such a case, the implication of the pandemic generalized model, as for instance that arising from COVID-19, establishes the approach to pandemic treatment and progressive control. Such a control mechanism is like the dispensation of randomized control trials (RCTs) within a given time period and application of various treatments. Such a treatment sets up proper choices of applicative instruments, methods, and policies for identifying effectiveness of control in the sense of science-economy-society moral inclusiveness. In the case of COVID-19 such process-based selection of treatments and controls were application of face masks, social distancing, lockdowns, and quarantine.

Time in the sense of inter-systemic process denotes repetitive accumulation of intra-systemic processes over blocks of time periods as experimental durations. An example in relation to COVID-19 is effective time period during the search for vaccines, oral medicine, anti-body tests, hygiene, cleanliness, sustained community wellbeing responsibilities, and repetition of the intra-system RCTs. Each of the blocks of time periods is analytically treated in respect of the entire abstracto-empirical methodology and the emergent models of repetitive inter-system RCT over spans of measured effects during such time periods. The resulting time-trajectories of intra-systemic IIE-learning become benchmarks of analytical facts and policy recommendations in sustainability over knowledge, pandemic vectors representing knowledge-induced space, and knowledge-induced time dimension. The degrees of effectiveness (complementarities) denoted by evaluated values of wellbeing indexes $\{\theta(\varepsilon), t(\theta(\varepsilon))\}$ can be read over time.

Figure 6.4 shows the intra-system and inter-system paths of consciousness-induced change in knowledge, space, and time dimensions. In the case of pandemic control as a special case, Figure 6.4 shows the most critical exogenously applied attribute of belief and good behaviour denoted by attributes $\{\varepsilon\}$ embodied in knowledge. Although exogenously applied in the continuum of sustainability with moral inclusiveness, by itself $\{\varepsilon\}$ is individually felt but cannot be quantitatively evaluated. Theoretically, $\{\varepsilon\}$ is abstractly subject to circular causation of its own through its embedding in the knowledge parameters and thereby in the knowledge-induced world-system, now generalized by various pandemic episodes. Figure 6.4 is shown without axes to imply its non-cardinal topological mathematical nature of the intrinsic mathematical non-Cartesian dynamics overall.

Conclusion

The experience of COVID-19 as a massive example of pandemic episode, and whose generalized consequences are poverty and social disempowerment, has brought to light the need for various types of attention on socio-economic development and changes in educational philosophy and in the nature of the generalized science-economy-society model of moral inclusiveness. From this study we learn that altogether new perspectives need to be formulated with enforceable policy, behavioural, and institutional perspectives in regional and global contexts. The important emphasis is to be given to the moral and social depth of imparting the new co-determined

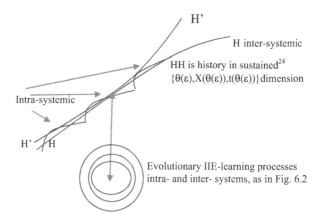

Figure 6.4 Topological manifestation of attributive induction of intra- and inter-systemic IIE-learning model of moral inclusiveness

multidisciplinary curricula in the complementary socio-scientific fields. The existing models of teaching and learning regarding pandemic governance are devoid of applying the moral and ethical values as endogenous forces of moral and social inclusiveness of wellbeing. The existing models of science-economy-society relations do not embody the moral elements as part of studying and 'treating' generalized forms of pandemic episodes. Thus, the new form of the science-economy-society model of moral inclusiveness must reform the traditional models by altogether new epistemic rethinking. Such versatile models ought to be taught, learnt, applied, and practised in the broadest domain of human activity and resource development for the wellbeing of all out of pandemic episodes in continued sustainability and for the consequences of pandemic episodes.

HH moves up or down in intra- and inter-systemic trajectories of pandemic episodes as $\varepsilon\uparrow\downarrow$, respectively, according to similar induced movements in $\theta(\varepsilon)$-values and its consequent effects on '$X(\theta(\varepsilon))$' over time, 't$(\theta(\varepsilon))$.'

Notes

1 Discussed in INET, July 2020 between Rob Johnson and Michael Sandel prior to publication of the book by Michel Sandel, *The Tyranny of Merit: What's Become of the Common Good?* Sept. 2020.
2 Ashford, R. & Shakespeare, R. (1999). *Binary Economics – the New Paradigm*, University Press of America, Lanham, MD.
3 Hayek, F.A. (1967). "The principles of liberal social order", in his *Studies in Philosophy, Politics and Economics*, The University of Chicago Press, Chicago, IL.

4 Becker, G.S. (1994). *Human Capital: A Theoretical and Empirical Analysis with Special Reference to Education*, Third Edition, The University of Chicago Press, Chicago, IL.

Schultz, T. (1971). *Investment in Human Capital: The Role of Education and of Research*, Free Press, New York.

5 Bowles, S. & Gintis, H. (1975). "The problem with human capital theory: A Marxian critique", *American Economic Review*, May.

6 Solow, R. (1980). *Growth Theory, an Exposition*, Oxford University Press, Oxford.

7 Romer, P.M. (1986). "Increasing returns and long-run growth", *Journal of Political Economy*, 94, pp. 1002–1037.

8 Romer, P.M. (1986). "Increasing returns and long-run growth", *Journal of Political Economy*, 94, pp. 1002–1037.

9 Friedman, M. (1992). *Capitalism and Freedom*, University of Chicago Press, Chicago.

10 South Commission. (1990). *The Challenge to the South*, Oxford University Press, Oxford.

11 Sen, A. (1999). "Functioning and well-being", in *Commodities and Capabilities*, Oxford University Press, New Delhi.

Sen, A. (1986). *Poverty and Famines, an Essay on Entitlement and Deprivation*, Clarendon Press, Oxford.

12 Nussbaum, M. (2011). *Creating Capabilities*, Harvard University Press, Cambridge, MA.

13 *Stanford Encyclopedia of Philosophy* (Oct. 3, 2016). "The capability approach".

14 Harsanyi, J.C. (1955). "Cardinal welfare, individualistic ethics, and interpersonal comparisons of utility", *Journal of Political Economy*, 63, pp. 309–321.

15 Westhues, A. (2006). *Canadian Social Policy: Issues and Perspectives*, Wilfrid Laurier University Press.

16 Jochem, S. (Jan. 2011). *Scandinavian Labour and Social Policy, Models for a Preventive Welfare State*, Friedrich-Ebert-Siftung, International Policy Analysis, Berlin, Germany.

17 Choudhury, M.A. (2014). "Chapter 6: Corporate social consciousness and responsibility with an ethico-economic idea of productivity and efficiency", in *Socio-Cybernetic Study of God and the World-System*, IGI-Inc., Philadelphia, PA.

18 Kaku, M. (2015). "Consciousness: A physicist's viewpoint", in his *The Future of the Mind*, Chapter 2, Anchor Book, New York, NY.

19 Commission on Global Governance. (1995). "Global civic ethic", in *Our Global Neighbourhood, a Report of the Commission on Global Governance*, Oxford University Press, New York.

20 Choudhury, M.A. (2020). "Unified model of global wellbeing as index of spirituality and socio-economic development: The Islamic economic approach", *Journal of Social Sciences*, 16: pp. 63–71.

21 $\vartheta = {}^{2}\sqrt{[\vartheta_1(\theta(\varepsilon))*\vartheta_2(\theta(\varepsilon))]}$ as simple geometric average without coefficients.

22 $W(\theta(\varepsilon)) = \Pi_{i,j,k,s,u,v}\,(Q_i.C_j.M_k.T_s.\vartheta_u.\vartheta_v)[\theta(\varepsilon)]$, along with the inter-variable circular causation relations and the empirical form of the joint and individual wellbeing function in $\{q(\varepsilon)\}$. The coefficients of the variables are dropped.

23 Wilson, E.O. (1998). *Consilience: The Unity of Knowledge*, Vantage Books, New York.

7 Selected reforms in business-pandemic studies to accord with the model of science-economy-society moral inclusiveness

Introduction

In this chapter we ask the following selected questions and answer them in the contrasting models of business decision-making and asset valuation: Can the utilitarian model of expected utility function have an endogenous ethical link with the pandemic human situation? Can the welfare function in its orientation of expected utility function endow an endogenous continuity and sustainability impact on the moral outlook of decision-making as it would thereby affect the pandemic situation? In contradistinction to these questions there is the unique and universal epistemic alternative to the evaluation of the wellbeing objective criterion in the light of moral inclusiveness of science-economy-society multi-disciplinary ensemble. The contradictory lesson is learnt in specific examples of business studies in terms of their traditional premise of economic rationality and the rationalism episteme. In such a priori versus a posteriori epistemic context there exists the dissociation between the a priori foundation of pure and imperative reason and the a posteriori reasoning of antinomy from the a priori moral episteme. Such a dissociative multidisciplinary understanding of moral inclusiveness is the primal cause of methodological independence between the moral and material domains of human experience. We have explained in this work that such methodological independence is the cause of moral exclusion and methodological individualism in pandemic episodes.

Possible revision of business studies in the framework of the model of moral inclusiveness

1 Utilitarian business decision-making: moral exclusion of business pandemic studies and its alternative of moral inclusiveness study

Following is the explanation of the nature of moral exclusion of pandemic episode in the utilitarian decision-making approach:

The continuously differentiable function, which is the unfailing property of the wellbeing function in endogenous ethical values (ε) inducing the knowledge variables (θ) like 'θ(ε)' has no presence in Taylor's Theorem applied to the utility function as follows:

The continuously differentiable function of the variable 'x,' 'f(x)' is expandable in the neighbourhood of 'c' in the following knowledge-induced form. It shows that at best in the mathematical context, the extendable continuously differentiable property, hence moral sustainability, is applicable in the dynamic knowledge-induced neighbourhood of $\{c(\theta(\varepsilon))\}$.

$$f(x(\theta(\varepsilon))) = [f(c) + (x-c)/1!*f'(c) + (x-c)^2/2!*f''(c) + \ldots$$
$$+ (x-c)^n/n!*f^n(c)][\theta(\varepsilon)] \qquad (7.1)$$

By replacing f(.) with the neoclassical economic and finance version (business decision-making) of utility function in risk (Var(x)) and return (cashflows, x) the expression (7.1) does not maintain its property of continuous differentiability in terms of $\{\theta(\varepsilon)\}$. Hence the property of moral sustainability as found in the IIE-learning version of the wellbeing function does not exist in the neoclassical conception of classroom and textbook orientation. Thereby, neoclassical economic and finance expression of utility in risk and return does not extend to $\{\theta(\varepsilon)\}$. The generalized theoretical form of expression (7.1) cannot therefore apply to the neoclassical form of utility function in risk and return. This neoclassical form always taught and pronounced in books and classroom business studies thereby dispels moral inclusiveness of risk and return. This is a permanent failure of existing business studies in all its pedagogical delivery originating from the primal episteme of unity of knowledge between the knowledge-induced variables.

The failure of neoclassical utility function in policy-theoretic aspects of decision-making with moral inclusiveness replaces the relationship between risk and return. This happens in substantive different ways in the case of the IIE-learning theory of wellbeing in unity of knowledge and its inter-variable induction, consequent to $\theta(\varepsilon)\uparrow$. The attitudinal marginalist property of utility tradeoff between risk and return is now replaced by complementary property between risk and return. This results from institutional organization of increasing risk-sharing. This in respect of the increasing number of shareholders with unit shareholding $(sh(\theta(\varepsilon)))$ and increasing output (returns, $x(\theta(\varepsilon))$) by focusing on the life-sustaining production and consumption activities, all together reduce the unit risk $(u(\theta(\varepsilon)) = Var(x(\theta(\varepsilon)))/sh(\theta(\varepsilon))*x(\theta(\varepsilon)))$. This in turn increases the expected returns. While the total risk may increase, unit risk declines. That is by circular causation between the endogenously interrelated variables of the wellbeing objective criterion dealt with throughout this book, the resulting following inter-causal relationship between risk and return in the framework of unity of knowledge applies to the problem of pandemic episode:

$$\theta(\epsilon)\uparrow \leftrightarrow (\mathbf{x}(\theta(\epsilon))\uparrow \leftrightarrow sh(\theta(\epsilon)))\uparrow \leftrightarrow u(\theta(\epsilon)))\downarrow.^1 \tag{7.2}$$

2   Utilitarian welfare function-based decision-making:[2] *moral exclusion in business-pandemic studies and its alternative of moral inclusiveness study*

We define the welfare function, $W(U_1, U_2, \ldots U_n)$, in terms of the aggregation of several utility functions, $\{U_i, i=1,2, \ldots, n\}$ in any of the following forms:

$$1 \quad W(U_1, U_2, \ldots U_n) = \Sigma_{i=1}^n \, \alpha_i \, U_i(x_i, Var(x_i)) \tag{7.3}$$

wherein the presence of knowledge variables $\{\theta(\epsilon)\}$ as endogenous embedding of the other variables and the additive coefficients, $\{\alpha_i\}$ remains dysfunctional. Moral and ethical effects on the utility functions and thereby the welfare function remain exogenous in nature. Thereby, all the properties of inter-variable methodological independence and the agential property of methodological individualism prevail between self, markets, and institutions. All the properties of utility maximization, thereby welfare maximization, discussed in respect of utilitarianism and premised in economic rationality and the episteme of rationalism as methodological dissociation between a priori reason and a posteriori reason prevail.

In the global pandemic sense, expression (7.3) can be implied to represent region-wide aggregate form of the welfare function in terms of the individual utilities of members of the global community. In the absence of moral inclusiveness in the utilitarian framework of science-economy-society having no endogenous effect of $\{\theta(\epsilon)\}$ on the multidisciplinary ensemble of variables, business pandemic studies with moral consciousness cannot be pursued. In this case all the properties of dissociative nature characterizing science, economy, and society cause moral exclusion in the study of business pandemic study. The specific case in this regard is the utilization of the dissociative multidisciplinary method that is made to address utilitarian welfare maximization in respect of the usual treatment of risk and return behaviour of business decision-making in choices of investments, and in capitalization of cash-flows on a global community scale.

Such a dissociative nature of regional welfare of pandemic resolution can be found in the realpolitik of vaccine manufacture and competition for trade access between so many countries. Some of these competing global members comprise the USA, Russia, China, India. Fidler writes on a similar problem of international sharing of knowledge on COVID-19 treatment and cure (Fidler, 2020)[3]. The consequences of such lack of global sharing causing the vast pandemic adverse effects in science-economy-society moral inclusiveness result in notoriously deadweight wellbeing losses.

$$2 \quad W(U_1, U_2, \ldots, U_n) = A * U_1 \alpha^{1} * U_2^{\alpha 2} \ldots * U_n^{\alpha n} \qquad (7.4)$$

With, $U_i = U_i(x_i, Var(x_i))$, $i = 1, 2, \ldots, n$. Bold symbols denote vectors

The identity of expression (7.4) to (7.3) is noted by converting into log-linear form denoted by lower case symbols as

$$w = a + \Sigma_{i=1}^{n} u_i(x_i, Var(x_i)) \qquad (7.5)$$

The critical study of expression (7.5) regarding the modelling of moral inclusiveness of business decision-making and valuation of assets is identical with the section 1 given earlier. The continuation of this kind of business study remains incapable of policy-theoretic application to business-pandemic case study. This prosaic study is thereby changed into an altered analytic of moral inclusiveness of risk and return study by the complementary study in the multidisciplinary field induced by the episteme of unity of knowledge. Such a universality and uniqueness of the business-pandemic study of moral inclusiveness by the implications of expression (7.2) opens up a broad horizon in the fields of business ethics, epistemic conceptualization as by the ontology of unity of knowledge, and phenomenological application of sustainability in the treatment and resolution of pandemic problems for wellbeing.

3 Matrix portfolio analysis of business-pandemic study and its alternative analytic model of moral inclusiveness

In the light of the business-pandemic study in moral inclusiveness of multidimensional elements of the continuous knowledge, space, and time passage of investments in the securities of good things of life over time, $z_s(\theta) = (\theta_s, x_s(\theta_s), t(\theta_s))$ over diverse securities $(s=1,2,\ldots,n)$ in the portfolio of securities, $P(\theta, X(\theta), t(\theta))$. We write, $P(\theta, x(\theta), t(\theta)) = \{s(\theta)\}_{s=1,2,\ldots,n}$. Each security, and thereby aggregate, the portfolio as a whole, is evaluated by means of its knowledge-induced cash-flows and decision-making process in the framework of IIE-learning processes. The valuation of securities in the portfolio have their respective wellbeing objective criterion $(w_s(\theta_s))$ and for the portfolio as a whole the wellbeing function is $W(w_s(\theta_s))$. Valuation of investments, cash-flows, and decision-making along the respective IIE-processes integrate in terms of the knowledge-induced $\{z_s(\theta_s)\}_{s=1,2,\ldots,n}$. In the case of business-pandemic studies the elements mentioned here denote those that are conducive to resolve pandemic problems along with promoting human incapability contra debilitating capability as explained earlier.

Table 7.1 displays the horizontal (intra-system) and vertical (inter-systems) securities to portfolio IIE-learning processes. The table explains this process. The following symbols denote

$r_s(\theta_s)$: real return from investments and cash-flows of life-fulfilling things of life, such as restructuring of economic structures towards human capability and business-pandemic study complementing the multidisciplinary parts in the science-economy-society model of moral inclusiveness.

$P_s(r_s(\theta))$: probability for realizing '$r_s(\theta)$' across different socio-scientific states of the specific securities, $s = 1, 2, \ldots, n_1$.

Thereby, the portfolio real rate of return '$r(\theta)$' is calculated by

$$r(\theta) = [\Sigma_{s=1}^{n1} P_s {}^* r_s][\theta]$$

A_{st} denote cash-flows net of cash-flows in security 's' over time 't' arising from business-pandemic related securitization of the portfolio (θ_s). Table 7.1 implies that such net cash-flows and the expected real rates of return are continuous so as to establish sustainability of the IIE-learning processes in the case of business-pandemic study. Thereby, the discursive base of decision-making between self, markets, and institutions as of science-economy-society in moral exclusiveness is a simultaneously continuous

Table 7.1 Business-pandemic formulation of multivariate asset valuation in respect of moral inclusiveness

s=n; time	0	1 . . . . . . n_1
θ-induced	A_{n0}	$A_{n1} + A_{n0}(1 + r_n(\theta_n)) \ldots A_{n,n1} + A_{n,n-1}$
		$(1 + r_n(\theta_n)) + A_{n0}(1 + r_n(\theta_n))^{n1} = n\text{-}Terminal\ Valuation$
Investments,		↑
Cash-flows,		n-Terminal Valuation $w_{1t}(\mathbf{zn}(\theta_n))$, at each t=1,2,. .,$n_1$
Decision-making.		
. . . .		}Portfolio, $W(\mathbf{ws}(z_s(\boldsymbol{\theta}s)))$
s=1; time	0	1 . . . . . . n_1
θ-induced	A_{10}	$A_{11} + A_{10}(1 + r_1(\theta_1)) \ldots A_{1n1} + A_{1n-1}$
		$(1 + r_1(\theta_1)) + A_{10}(1 + r_1(\theta_1))^{n1} = 1\text{-}Terminal\ Valuation$
Investments,	↑	
Cash-flows,		1-Terminal Valuation $w_{1t}(\mathbf{z1}(\theta_1))$, at each t=1,2,. .,$n_1$
Decision-making		

Table 7.2 Construction of business-pandemic portfolio wellbeing by securitization in the good choices of normalization away from pandemic mutation

Time			
Securities	1	2	... n_1
1	$a_{11}*w_{11}$	$a_{12}*w_{12}$	... $a_{1,n1}*w_{1,n1}$
2	$a_{21}*w_{21}$	$a_{22}*w_{22}$	... $a_{2,n1}*w_{2,n1}$
$\cdots\cdots$			
n	$a_{n1}*w_{n1}$	$a_{n2}*w_{n2}$	... $a_{n,n1}*w_{n,n1}$
Portfolio wellbeing in terms of security-time specific log-linear wellbeing functions of pandemic resolution $W(\theta)$	$\Sigma_{s=1}{}^{n}a_{s1}*w_{s1}$ $= W_1(w_{s1}(\theta))$	$\Sigma_{s=1}{}^{n}a_{s2}*w_{s2}$ $= W_2(w_{s2}(\theta))$	... $\Sigma_{s=1}{}^{n}a_{s,n1}*w_{s,n1}$ $= W_{n1}(w_{s,n1}(\theta))$
Product version of the portfolio wellbeing function in terms of security-time	$W_1(w_{s1}(\theta_{s1}))$ $= \Pi_{s1}w_{s1}{}^{as1}(\theta_{s1})$	$W_2(w_{s2}(\theta_{s2}))$ $= \Pi_{s2}w_{s2}{}^{as2}(\theta_{s2})$	... $W_{n1}(w_{s,n1}(\theta_{s,n1}))$ $= \Pi_{s,n1}w_{s,n1}{}^{as,n1}(\theta_{s,n1})$

activity intra- and inter-systems of securities to contribute to business-pandemic characteristic study of valuation by means valuation of the securities and portfolio wellbeing functions.

Bold symbols denote multivariate vectors at each time period of valuation of wellbeing functions. The time period specific portfolio-wide valuations of securities can be represented in the following table. The portfolio-wide valuations of securities are expressed by the product function of security valuations by time periods to display the IIE-learning non-linear portfolio wellbeing function as shown next. The coefficients $(a_{st}(\theta))$ so existing for securities by specific time periods signify the effectiveness of moral inclusiveness in the pandemic resolution. Here is the formalism of portfolio wellbeing in terms of the weighted log-linear security wellbeing functions $(w_{st}(\theta))$, $s = 1, 2, .., n; t = 1, 2, ..., n_1$.

Table (7.2) explains the security-diversification by IIE-learning processes of a business-pandemic portfolio for pandemic normalization out of mutation in respect of the episteme of unity of knowledge and its induced good choices by means of 'θ_{st}' resulting in the multivariate choices of '$z(\theta_{st})$.'

Conclusion: business-pandemic elements in a new approach to business studies

The surge of COVID-19 pandemic episode has inundated the human ecological world-system. Thereby, deepening poverty, deprivation, unemployment, and moral exclusion in the ensuing science-economy-society dissociative way of pursuing an archaic idea of multidisciplinarity have made human possibilities unsustainable (Heilbroner, 1991).[4] Our study in risk and return in this section points out that the prosaic way of treating such a utilitarian study in the continuing bookish and classroom studies cannot address the pandemic malaise as moral issues for resolution. The classroom and books, new epistemic pursuit of learning of business studies in conjunction with the moral world-system of multidisciplinary perspectives to complement risk and return in developing life-fulfillment and sharing economies must seek out the alternative ways of assuming risk and return in complementary shared and joint ventures. Similar business-pandemic studies overarch all specific courses and subject areas.

Risk avoidance and utilitarian economic rationality and its epistemic rationalism for maximizing the utility objective in cash-flows are altered in the wellbeing perspective of complementary interrelations between risk and return. This alternative approach risk and return taking is pointed out by the result of expression (7.2). The underlying multidisciplinary model of moral inclusiveness in the complementary ensemble of science-economy-society now formulates analytical and self, markets, institutional consciousness approach to the study of business courses. This approach results in the study of the real world-system of pandemic resolution by means of the previously mentioned kind of complementary interaction and methodological coexistence. Thereby, the bookish and attitudinal properties of competition for scarce resources and human-market-institutional psyche of methodological individualism of the genre of studying maximizing utilitarian behaviour must be modelled in the moral framework of the new episteme. This is unity of knowledge embodied in the wellbeing objective criterion of pandemic resolution along with its methodological details.

Notes

1 By referring to expression (7.1) with $\theta(\varepsilon)$-induction of the utility function now appearing as wellbeing function $(f(x,u)[\theta(\varepsilon)])$, in terms of the attitudinal properties included in expression (7.2), we can write,

$$0 < \overset{>0}{\mathrm{df/d}\theta(\varepsilon)} = (\overset{>0}{\partial f/\partial x})^*(\mathrm{dx}(\theta(\varepsilon)))/\mathrm{d}(\theta(\varepsilon)))) + ((\overset{<0}{\partial f/\partial u})^*((\overset{<0}{\mathrm{du}(\theta(\varepsilon))}/\mathrm{d}(\theta(\varepsilon)))] > 0$$

along the IIE-learning sustainability path.
See Jean, W.H. (1970). *The Analytical Theory of Finance, A Study of the Investment Decision Process of the Individual and the Firm*, Holt, Rinehart and Winston, Inc., New York.

2 Hammond, P.J. (1989). "On reconciling Arrow's theory of social choice with Harsanyi's fundamental utilitarianism", in G.R. Feiwel, ed. *Arrow and the Foundation of the Theory of Economic Policy*, pp. 179–221, Macmillan, London.

3 Fidler, D.P. (Aug. 13, 2020). "To fight a new Coronavirus: The COVID-19 Pandemic, political herd immunity, and global health jurisprudence", *Chinese Journal of International Law*, https://doi.org/10.1093/chinesejil/jmaa016

"Lamentations abound that political actions across the international system have disrupted pandemic cooperation and damaged international law. The World Health Organization (WHO) – the center of gravity for international health cooperation – confronts political and health crises. Other venues for cooperation, including the UN Security Council and the Group of 7, have not been productive."

4 Heilbroner, R.L. (1991). *An Inquiry into the Human Prospect*, W.W. Norton, New York, NY.

8   Conclusion

Future pandemic model beyond COVID-19

The future of moral inclusiveness in the aftermath of pandemic episode

The conclusion thereby derived is this: the future of pandemic control in its generalized form cannot be treated, cured, and resolved by using the existing methodological approach. There is no epistemic basis to premise such methodology on complementary endogenous variables based on moral and ethical consciousness besides simply the science-economy-society materiality treatment. Our newly proposed model of complementarity between the science-economy-society moral inclusiveness also raises the following questions: 1 Are severe pandemic conditions expected to arise in the future that would require immediate preparations to combat? 2 If no great pandemic situation is expected to arise in the future, given the preparations completed for COVID-19, then will there be continued indifference to change during the regime of the ensuing Fourth Industrial Revolution (4IR)? 3 Will our proposed new model prepare the world towards pandemic security? Answers to these questions also reflect the various states of the science-economy-society global order and the need for moral consciousness in such multidisciplinary ensemble.

Pandemic occurrence of doomsday proportion will be caused by the unpreparedness of mankind in its intellection by ignorance of moral inclusiveness in 'everything.' The future pandemic doomsday scenario is presented by the Qur'an in light of the law of Tawhid, monotheistic unity of knowledge (Qur'an, 22:1–6).[2] The future pandemic episode of massive scale will indeed appear. Unless human beings are ready to modulate a morally inclusive world of unity of being and compassionate becoming the end will be cessation of human existence in the good earth.

Continuity of capitalist science-economy-society relationship during the near future of 4IR

The age of 4IR following on the aftermath of COVID-19 points out the unbalanced development of large corporation in comparison to the plight of microenterprises and small and medium-sized enterprises (SMEs), as for the case of Sweden in the industrialized world. While the overall unemployment rate in Sweden was 3.8% in 2019, the youth unemployment arising from their adverse effect of COVID-19 in Europe in general with which Sweden intensely trades, stood at 21% in 2020. In the developing world with the case of Bangladesh, young women's unemployment rate in the predominant garments-producing sector was 25%. This high rate combines with the already existing high unemployment rate of youth. Such wide gaps in unemployment between the corporate sector and microenterprises and their youth potential labor force point to the future continuing structure of development during 4IR. Consequently, the capitalist fervor of economic development will intensify in the near future. The funding aspects by way of grants, loans, social security, and microcredits will increase from government and private sector via CSR programs. Yet these aspects of exogenous funding for survival out of COVID-19 times will not enhance the productive and innovative possibilities within a changed science-economy-society structure of distribution of value-added between the corporate industrial sector and the rural sector.

Quoted section from the work of Stockholm School of Economics[3] states the following condition of enterprise and labor-market effect corresponding to Sweden. This example is reflective of the general capitalistic trend of all growth-led countries be they developed or developing countries (Pickety, 2017):[4]

Swedish corporatist model, to which 4IR general capitalist socio-scientific scenario will identify, particularly on the labor market, with two aspects.

> Firstly, traditional layoffs of full-time workers and the retraining and re-employment in new and growing export industries is less likely to be successful. Secondly, both the private and public segments of the infrastructure in Sweden are catering to large and export-oriented corporations, leaving microenterprises and SMEs in a comparatively disadvantaged situation.

The Stockholm School of Economics working paper points out that the COVID-19 pandemic is akin to a massive natural disaster. Like such disasters the COVID-19 pandemic leaves behind unprecedented economic and social adversities that become difficult to recover from, at least in the short run. The Indonesian Aceh tsunami took eight years for recovery from its destruction (World Bank, 2012).[5] In the developed countries as well, the US Federal Emergency Management Agency reports that only 60% of companies survive a natural disaster, and an additional 25% disappear within the first year after natural disaster. Far worsened statistics are reported by the US Small Business Administration. It found that over 90% of companies fail within two years following adverse impact of natural disaster. Furthermore, for the developed and peaceful countries such as Sweden in the European continent, the COVID-19 pandemic consequences in Sweden may cause the collapse of hundreds of thousands of SMEs and the erosion of large proportions of jobs and incomes, particularly among the youth in the microenterprise sector. The result of such long-term adversities proves that in the near future following COVID-19, 4IR will be unequally posed for the benefit of the corporate sector, even of the rich countries. Even the long-term recovery of the strain of the rich but corporate-oriented economies globally on the general welfare and micro-finance funding will be unprecedented. Thereby, the social benefits to the unemployed, youth, marginalized groups, and the static state of the corporate world-system will strain the differentiated science-economy-society situation against the wellbeing of the deprived. With the real value-added and earned income eroding in quantity and with the constraint in public and corporate financing the enterprise and marginalized households to sustain themselves will be deprived of the general social security, grants, loans, and welfare financing. The outlook for social and moral inclusiveness in the capitalist world-system of 4IR will therefore be increasingly less benefiting for the marginalized groups. 4IR will continue to pursue the presently prevailing model of the unequal distribution of resources between the corporate (rich world-system) and the microenterprises (deprivation of the poor world-system). More of the resources according to this mode of unequal distribution will be held by the industrialized sectors and economies at the exacerbation of the deprived sectors and of the developing countries. Trade, innovation, and prosperity in such a state of the world economy and its members will suffer because of the erosion of the ratification of development left behind in the aftermath of pandemic ravages, exemplified particularly by COVID-19.

An indifferent outlook of the pandemic future

The *Time* magazine article (15 May 2017), "The World Is Not Ready for the Next Pandemic," paints a gloomy picture on the pandemic shape of things to come. Causes for an indifferent world to recurrent pandemic episode in the near future can be deduced from the prevailing human negligence towards lockdown, social distancing, face masks, and consumption habits mostly to be found in the United States and China, respectively. Indeed, human behavioural and psychological conducts must be reformed in the first place to combine with science-economy-society-wide moral reform. There is complacence on this front by an indifferent population worldwide based on reliance in medical discoveries. But such a hope is dashed off by the failure of any new discovery of treatment by vaccines and medical services beyond what presently exist.

Many causes will militate in support of the possibility of the near next pandemic episode. Some of these are the following: the inevitable conditions of globalization by populations frequently moving across different geographical conditions make it likely for viral migrations and mutations. A looming case of unease is regarding the possibility of outburst of near future pandemic episodes on the scarcity and thereby competition for the financial resource and technological sharing at affordable cost by different end users of the industrialized and developing countries.

It is surmised that a severe outburst of the pandemic bird flu called H7N9 could cost $4 trillion. On the other hand, the immensely increasing military expenditure by $54 billion in the US would cut down necessary development and application proportions when the next pandemic strikes. So, in all, Michael Osterholm of the Center for Infectious Disease Research and Policy at the University of Minnesota predicts a power keg awaiting on top of the future pandemic episodes.

An alarming failure of predicting and advanced halting of the next pandemic is our absence of knowledge on the precise origin of COVID-19. Only the symptoms are known to identify the viral disease and to apply treatments thereby. It thereby remains unknown whether COVID-19 and subsequent pandemic episodes arise from certain kinds of animals and birds, their meat consumptions, and then migrate to humans. In the absence of knowing the specific origins of the pandemic outburst, it is impossible to develop the appropriate kinds of medicinal cure, treatments, and the precisely needed vaccines. Consequently, the effectiveness of predicting and halting the viral pandemic consumption, production, and livelihood and enforcing global institutional policies by the common will of development organizations to ban the inflicted consumption and production and their viral sources are required. Identification and enforcement of barriers to consumption, production, and distribution by market processes are difficult though in the face of a divided multicultural human habitation. Even as it stands today, the prevalence of COVID-19 has caused division and differences between the US and China on a global concerted approach towards controlling the pandemic.

Remedial approach for future pandemic situation

The mortal world and all its animate and inanimate entities will always be exposed to face uncertainties of life and death. Among such eventualities will be the repeated occurrence of pandemic. Along with this will recur the vicissitudes of existence. Therefore, the curative and scenarios of a future pandemic situation must not be placed within an optimal model of control of pandemic episodes and their consequences. On the other hand, this work has argued that human prospects of the future rest not on an optimal world of plenitude. Rather, the future of all matters in the shortest term and the long term is explained by the realistic model of learning to maintain in sustainability the viable wellbeing of all entities. Thus, the future prospect of existence ought to be a coexistent world-system of interactive (discursive), integrative (consensual), and ever-learning (evolutionary) socio-scientific order by virtue of the episteme of unity of knowledge for the collectively determined good things of life and avoidance of the harmful ones. The centrepiece of this form of human realization is possible and morally legitimate. The ontological origin, purpose, and conduct of life and existence are premised on a morally thoughtful and rightful pursuit of the good and neighbourly agreeable things. These are morally good and of wellbeing generating by virtue of their shared nature in the comity of nations and communities.

The participatory imminence of the IIE-learning model of science-economy-society wellbeing with endogenously affecting variables of moral inclusiveness reflects the very episteme of unity of knowledge as complementary interrelations. This is formally explained and implemented via the evaluation of the wellbeing objective criterion by the large system of circular causation equations comprising the wellbeing generating endogenous variables. The end of this empirical application of epistemic thought is the positivistic, policy, and institutional quantitative measure of the knowledge-induced wellbeing objective criterion that is analytically stated in its formalism. This characteristic of the model of science-economy-society moral inclusiveness in a coexisting human aspiration and existence is thereby a large-scale computerized model of the future pandemic situation and of the future ensuing era of morally inclusive change. The resulting model of the future control of pandemic situation is therefore a multidimensional, holistic pairing between the episteme of moral actualization and materiality. It is the soul-mind-matter moral representation in the wellbeing objective criterion. It is this objective function along with its generality and details of construction and functioning that establishes the overall scenario of future pandemic to control and live with even in the non-optimal world of human shortcoming.

Figure 8.1 shows where lies the human construction and regulation towards the human future of pandemic control. The imperfections of the

Table 8.1 The convergence of science-economy-society moral inclusiveness model for future pandemic control

The optimal model of pandemic future	The learning model (IIE) of pandemic future	Convergence to moral inclusiveness
First is the 4IR-model of optimal state of industrialization by means of the existing model of capitalist (neoclassical) economic growth having no explicit moral inclusiveness. Second is complacence on the existing situation of indifference by relying on the present financial power and surrender of industrialized countries to their economic power and scientific discoveries.	Consciously (endogenously) including the moral and social values of caring, sharing, and responsibility: change towards conscious need for moral framing up of a robust model of human resource development by moral-material embedding to be practised in teaching, pedagogy, research, and reformation of educational programs and policies	Examples: Sztompka, P.[6] Theory of Social Becoming; Hawley, A.[7] Human Ecology. World Bank,[8]"Social Inclusion." Sustainable Development Goals. Computerization of the large-scale model of wellbeing with large systems of survey data on science-economy-society-wide moral inclusiveness.[9]

previously mentioned approaches towards a solely materialistic outlook of pandemic control are shown in Table 8.1 to inevitably change directions towards attaining a workable model of abstracto-empirical epistemic form in terms of the wellbeing objective criterion. Indeed, the regime of COVID-19 is just one case of growing realization of the great multidisciplinary complexity of a system understanding of the issues under study in generality and particulars. The future pandemic problem must be cast in a multidisciplinary worldview of evolutionary learning to attain higher levels of materiality and moral inclusiveness with the analytical insight of the consciously knowledge-induced embedded world-system. The state of future pandemic episode ought to be studied and the multidisciplinary worldview developed with the full epistemic outlook and its possible instruments and institutional change (Wallerstein, 1998).[10]

An example of restructuring for science-economy-society moral inclusiveness

The endogenous nature of restructuring the future model of pandemic control, treatment, and cure is based on a comprehensive alteration of the existing economic and social framework of growth that promotes marginal rate of substitution between all forms of goods, services, and resources. The contrary model is premised on pervasive complementarities between the good choices all taken up within the objective of wellbeing. We now design a particular form of economic and social model that is premised on and continues to sustain the pervasively complementary inter-variable relations between the good choices while avoiding the unwanted ones for the objective of controlling the pandemic situation by the framework of such choices. Thereby, the epistemic outlook of unity of knowledge remains in consilience with the scientific, economic, and social entities. Here are the words of Parramore (2020)[11] that cast human future of uncertainty despite the clamor of scientific feat:

> But in this season of shattered expectations, a virus blows up our best-laid plans and mocks our carefully crafted models. When the future catches us unawares, anxiety surges. Right now, millennials are worried. Teachers are worried. Retirees are worried. The rich are worried. Hell, even Donald Trump is getting worried.

We take the example of the life-fulfillment wellbeing function arising from the complementary agri-industry based consumption and production menus in the economy-wide sense. Along with such an industrial structure are also the complementary labor force, its entrepreneurial characteristic, sustainability attributes of cultural and spiritual values that deepen communitarian empathy, clean living, and environmental coexistence. The nature of consumption and production can be so utilized and managed as to commercialize life-sustaining medicine and healthy artefacts of life. Herbal medicinal system, prophetic medicinal system (Zakaria, 6 April 2020),[12] and reducing pharmaceutical toxic waste in medicine production and consumption through their complexity and expensive chemical dispensation are examples that establish ecological harmony while they promote wellbeing.

An extended result in input-output matrix related to circular causation relations of moral inclusiveness

To make the circular causation system of equations fully compliant with the Input-Output Matrix we simply make the assumption that a part of any variable remains related to itself while the rest is related with the other variables. Thereby,

$$\ln x_i(\theta(\varepsilon)) = [\text{constants}]_i[\theta(\varepsilon)] + \Sigma_j(b_{ij}*\ln x_{ij})[\theta(\varepsilon)]; \ i,j = 1,2,\ldots \quad (8.8)$$

Expression (8.7) can be written as

$$[\ln x_i(\theta(\varepsilon))] = \|I-A(\theta(\varepsilon))\|^{-1}*[\text{constants}][\theta(\varepsilon)], \quad (8.9)$$

where, $A(\theta(\varepsilon)) = [a_{ij}(\theta(\varepsilon))]$, i, j = 1, 2, . . .

By the epistemic property of pervasive complementarities in the science-economy-society extant of moral inclusiveness, $a_{ij}(\theta(\varepsilon))) > 0$, i,j = 1,2, . . . signifying inter-sectoral and inter-variable organic pairing. The sustainability of condition for such a continuous and broadest extant of inter-variable complementarities is the requirement for development resources to be permanently augmented as by the variables shown in expression (8.1) and by the continuous sustainability of IIE-processes both intra-system and inter-systems over time and varieties. The inference thereby is that the input-output coefficients, meaning also the inter-variable dynamic partial elasticity coefficients, $a_{ij}(\theta(\varepsilon))) > 0$, i, j = 1,2, . . . are not fixed coefficients as in the usual case of Input-Output Model. Furthermore, in Figure 6.4 the IIE-learning trajectory H'H' implies for each $\theta(\varepsilon)\uparrow \Leftrightarrow a_{ij}(\theta(\varepsilon)))\uparrow$. Therefore, the result is $(d/d\theta(\varepsilon))(a_{ij}(\theta(\varepsilon))) > 0$.

The vector of variables of wellbeing expression (8.1) can be expanded by introducing many more variables. Among these there would be the financing variables as of social microenterprises. Examples in this respect are microcredit financing, participative financing instruments, and interest-free financing that would organically complement the financial sector and real economy sector via the monetary sector and its resource mobilization instruments. There is no end to these instruments that can complement the entire science-economy-society multidisciplinary ensemble with moral inclusiveness. The promising sector in such an ensemble comprises the life-sustaining productive activities of the rural social economy. The structure of such activities is exemplified by the linkages between the joint production related systems. Examples of such participative systems are the labor market, investment, entrepreneurship, technological diversity, conscious corporate social responsibility, clean consumption, and their production. Upon these undertakings there are the behavioural psychology and communitarian conduct of living, and many such preferences of clean and responsible coexisting life. Indeed, charity begins at home for markets and society at large (Choudhury, 1996).[13] And indeed, the agricultural sector is the one with the widest extant of sectoral and life-fulfilling linkages producing wellbeing for all. This encompasses self, family, community, nation, and the global entirety. Such pervasively complementary linkages are generated by the continuous jointness of economic, social, and moral activities arising from the rural sector. The rural sector comprises further jointness of such activities with the appropriate manufacturing, secondary, service, and tertiary sectors. In the earlier formalism, this state of the sectoral input-output is projected by

$$\theta(\varepsilon)\uparrow \Leftrightarrow a_{ij}(\theta(\varepsilon)))\uparrow; (d/d\theta(\varepsilon))(a_{ij}(\theta(\varepsilon))) > 0; i, j = 1, 2, . . . \qquad (8.10)$$

The shape of jointness of rural sector complementary linkages

Figure 8.1 is a composite diagram that explains how phases of jointness by output (I), labor (II), investment (III), and technology (IV) with many more of similar segments interconnect by IIE-learning science-economy-society model of moral inclusiveness. This sectoral interrelationship occurs continuously by circular causation evaluation cycles of sustainability. The activities interrelate and expand by organic complementarities as shown. Multisectoral diffusion of joint product is studied by Buckner et al. (2019).[14]

Symbols: I denotes joint sectoral output. II denotes labor market complementary to I. III denotes investment complementary with I and II. IV denotes technological diversity complementary with I, II, and III. Their expansionary dynamics of inter-sectoral jointness is denoted by evolutionary circles moving outwards under the continuous impact of $\{\theta(\varepsilon)\}$ with $\{\theta(\varepsilon)\}\uparrow \Leftrightarrow \{\varepsilon\}\uparrow$. This whole complementary evolution by unity of knowledge comprises the meaning of sustainability and is explained by the expanding squares. This dynamic signifies expression (8.10). This property is further conveyed by expression (8.11).

$$\theta(\varepsilon)\uparrow \Leftrightarrow a_{ij}(\theta(\varepsilon))\uparrow; (d/d\theta(\varepsilon))(a_{ij}(\theta(\varepsilon))) > 0; i,j = 1,2,\ldots \qquad (8.11)$$

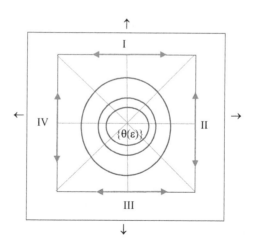

Figure 8.1 Interconnectedness by joint science-economy-society moral inclusiveness activities driven by $\{\theta(\varepsilon)\}$

Conclusion: policy-theoretic perspective

We have learnt important lessons in this work that are not usually imparted elsewhere in respect of any study on a pandemic episode and its ravaging effects. This is particularly true of the unprecedented maladies that today's humankind has fearfully faced during the yet continuing COVID-19 episode. This study has emphasized that deep human illness in all its forms and which will be contracted in the future pandemic episodes, will not be bereft of essential moral values that embed human consciousness and occurrences of diseases equally out of human indifference. Thus, consciousness and practice of values and deprivation caused by the absence of moral values embedded in science-economy-society fullness are culminating syndromes of illness in all its enervating forms. To get over the dark recurrence of future pandemic episodes and diseases the moral element of science-economy-society ensemble must be seriously and inevitably included, learnt, and positively practiced in the epistemic theory of pandemic as a moral-material problem along with its appropriate science-economy-society multidimensional aspects.

First thereby, this work has put forth the essentially required epistemic change in the socio-scientific theory of disease, medicine, and human activities by the moral inclusion with the rest. In such a study it is not enough to claim ethical conduct by way of human services rendered by medical science and policy-theoretic institutions. These attributes are consequences, yet not origins, of the blessed seat of moral values that arise from common human sharing. They are as much concepts as consciously applied at the highest echelons of scientific discoveries of soul, mind, and matter attributes framed in unity of knowledge at the epistemic foundations (Nasr, 1992).[15]

By the same representation of human values arising from its epistemic roots of unity of knowledge, the lesson of such unity of being and becoming in the total meaning of functioning of consciousness ought to be analytically understood in 'everything.' The field of 'everything' comprises the topological wholeness of choices of the good things and activities at the shunning of those that contradict the episteme of unity of knowledge. Examples of the imminent values to be embedded in soul, mind, and matter are first moral consciousness of organic unity of relations among all entities, animate and inanimate. Thus, we use the term socio-scientific totality and the principle of organic complementarities by self and systemic participation.

In the same way as explosive mutations breed pandemic so also the selfishness of methodological individualism breeds the cast of social division. This in turn causes the rupture in the capability to derive and sustain a world-system of moral simplicity that brings wellbeing to all. Wellbeing becomes the objective criterion to attain by continuous learning as evolutionary human trait. The episteme of unity of knowledge is thereby the foundation of the new outlook of the pandemic treatment model of moral inclusiveness of science-economy-society.

The same inextricable epistemic foundation of the worldview encompassing soul, mind, and matter as the framework of consciousness premised in unity of knowledge ought to reformulate all of human activities. This work has pointed out the urgent need for reformulating the socio-scientific curriculums by the morally conducive teaching, research, pedagogy, and globally collective dissemination of ideas, formalism, and structure of learning for the common good. The attainment of resulting wellbeing as the objective criterion is thereby actualized. Imam Fakhruddin Razi's model (Noor, 1998)[16] of worshipping world-system (ubudiyyah) is one such example. Another example of the evolutionary learnt model of self-actualized wellbeing with globally social meaning is of Abraham Maslow's (1968).[17]

Need for structural socio-scientific change with moral inclusiveness

This work has argued that structural change into participative socio-economic development between agricultural life-sustaining focus and rural-based industries will be emphasized at the exclusion of environment and wellbeing depriving activities. In such a socio-economic development orientation the principle of organic unity between sectors and the utilization of the good factors of goods and services in production, consumption, and distribution are sustained in the midst of moral inclusiveness.

By the similar importance of high finance to combat future pandemic episodes, the moral values ought to be introduced by developing and organizing such finances with the instruments that promote resources and their distribution and ownership among many for purposes of socio-economic equality, capability and functioning, and poverty alleviation. New orientation to monetary, fiscal, human resource development, trade, and environmental security policies for socio-economic development are required. Yet, the IMF conditionality and World Bank's structural adjustment program for developing countries have proved to be in favour of capitalistic market economic orientation with its neoclassical growth focus in market and privatization venue (Pettinger, 2019; Oppong, 2014).[18]

Market-based transformation of developing economies for achieving degrees of wellbeing by privatization and institutional enforcement is not an altogether unacceptable approach. The difference between free and fair market venues is the result of an ethically learning privatization approach.

The important element of the underlying policies promoting fair market transformation is based on a discursive participative approach. While this practice is an epistemic worldview it is also a practical and applied undertaking in community and institution based on a global scale of coexistence. Here the epistemic formalism and application towards attaining wellbeing by market-institution discursive transformation fully lends itself to the predominating IIE-learning model of this work. The concrescence gained in the emergent policy-theoretic, market-institution, epistemic model of fair and free transformation is of global undertaking towards upholding the unitary worldview of process and reality (Whitehead, 1978).[19] This formalism indeed is the all-encompassing worldview of pandemic control by science-economy-society model of moral inclusiveness with unifying multidisciplinary ensemble.[20]

Notes

1 Inglott, P.S. (1990). "The rights of future generations: Some socio-philosophical considerations", in S. Busuttil, E. Agius, P.S. Inglott & T. Macelli, eds. *Our Responsibilities Towards Future Generations*, pp. 17–27, Foundation for International Studies & UNESCO, Malta.

2 Qur'an (22:1–4): "O mankind, fear your Lord. Indeed, the convulsion of the [final] Hour is a terrible thing. On the Day you see it every nursing mother will be distracted from that [child] she was nursing, and every pregnant woman will abort her pregnancy, and you will see the people [appearing] intoxicated while they are not intoxicated; but the punishment of Allah is severe. And of the people is he who disputes about Allah without knowledge and follows every rebellious devil. It has been decreed for every devil that whoever turns to him – he will misguide him and will lead him to the punishment of the Blaze. O People, if you should be in doubt about the Resurrection, then [consider that] indeed, We created you from dust, then from a sperm-drop, then from a clinging clot, and then from a lump of flesh, formed and unformed – that We may show you. And We settle in the wombs whom We will for a specified term, then We bring you out as a child, and then [We develop you] that you may reach your [time of] maturity. And among you is he who is taken in [early] death, and among you is he who is returned to the most decrepit [old] age so that he knows, after [once having] knowledge, nothing. And you see the earth barren, but when We send down upon it rain, it quivers and swells and grows [something] of every beautiful kind. That is because Allah is the Truth and because He gives life to the dead and because He is over all things competent.

3 Engström, P., Altafi, S., Karlberg, G. & Nachemson-Ekvall, S. (n.d. memeo). "New funding for microenterprises and SMEs", Stockholm School of Economics. www.hhs.se/en/research/sweden-through-the-crisis/new-funding-for-micro-enterprises-and-smes/, visited July 24, 2020.

4 Pickety, T., trans. Goldhammer, A. (2017). *Capital in the Twenty-First Century*, Belknap Press of Harvard University Press, Boston, MA.

5 World Bank (Dec. 26, 2012) report. "Indonesia: A reconstruction chapter ends eight years after the tsunami". www.worldbank.org/en/news/feature/2012/12/26/

indonesia-reconstruction-chapter-ends-eight-years-after-the-tsunami, visited July 24, 2020.

6 Sztompka, P. (1991). *Society in Action, The Theory of Social Becoming*, The University of Chicago Press, Chicago, IL.

7 Hawley, A. (1986). *Human Ecology*, University of Chicago Press, Chicago, IL.

8 World Bank. "Social Inclusion". www.worldbank.org/en/topic/social-inclusion, visited July 24, 2020.

9 Intelligent Infrastructure (July 13, 2020). "The impact of COVID-19 on the global digital economy". www.cio.com/article/3566142/the-impact-of-covid-19-on-the-global-digital-economy.html, visited July 24, 2020.

10 Wallerstein, I. (1998). "Spacetime as the basis of knowledge", in O.F. Bordo, ed. *People's Participation, Challenges Ahead*, pp. 43–62, Apex Press, New York, NY.

11 Parramore, L. (July 29, 2020). "Is Silicon Valley nudging us towards an authoritarian future?", *Technology & Innovation*, INET.

12 Zakaria, A. (April 6, 2020). "Prophet Muhammad's guidance for the prevention of Coronavirus", *Discover Islam Kuwait Portal*.

13 Choudhury, M.A. (1996). "Markets as a system of social contracts", *The International Journal of Social Economics*, 23:1.

14 Buckner, M., Wood, R., Moran, D., Kuschnig, N., Wieland, H., Maus, V. & Borner, J. (2019). "FABIO – the construction of the food and agricultural Biomass Input-Output model", *Environmental Science & Technology*, 53, pp. 11302–11312.

15 Nasr, S.H. (1992). "The Gnostic tradition", in his *Science and Civilization in Islam*, Barnes & Noble, New York, NY.

16 Noor, H.M. "Razi's human needs theory and its relevance to ethics and economics", *Humanomics*, 14:1, pp. 59–96.

17 Maslow, A.H. (1968). *Towards a Psychology of Being*, Van Nostrand Reinhold, New York, NY.

18 Pettinger, T. (March 3, 2019). "Structural adjustment – definition and criticisms". www.economicshelp.org/blog/2139/economics/structural-adjustment/.
    Oppong, N.Y. (2014). "Failure of structural adjustment programmes in Sub-Saharan Africa: Policy design or policy implementation?", *Journal of Empirical Economics*, Research Academy of Social Sciences, 3:5, pp. 321–331.

19 Whitehead, A.N. (1978). *Process and Reality*, D.R. Griffin & D.W. Sherburne, eds. Free Press, New York.

20 *The New York Times* (May 8, 2020) quotes expert views on the future possible control of pandemic in the following words: "we can change the course of the pandemic – with our behavior, by balancing and coordinating psychological, sociological, economic and political factors."

Index

Note: Page numbers in *italics* indicate figures and page numbers in **bold** indicate tables.

134   *Index*

neoclassical economic growth:
disempowerment and 93–94;
educational policies and 93;
endogenous ethical development
and 95–97; imponderable
variables and 98; incapability
and 101–102; inequality and
92–93; macroeconomics and 67;
methodological individualism and
84, 94; pandemic treatment and
renormalization 94–95, *95*, 96–99;
poverty and 97–98
non-linear modelling 77–78, 80–82,
88n29
Nussbaum, M. 102

Organisation for Economic
Co-operation and Development
(OECD) 35
Osterholm, M. 121

pandemic control: consciousness-
induced change in 107, 127;
economic and social restructuring
for 3, 36, 123–124; methodological
individualism in xx, 118; science-
economy-society moral inclusiveness
and 64, 104–105, 122–123, **123**,
127–129, 130n20
pandemic episodes: consilience and
1; economic impact of 119–121;
epistemic methodology for xviii,
xix, xx; globalization and 121;
Islamic values and 13; mutation
and xviii, *xix*, 14; poverty and 36,
97, 99, 104–107; preparation for
118; prophetic guidance and 53n14;
recurrence of 120–122; religion and
22; social malaises and 4; Tawhidi
law and xviii, 33; wellbeing and 36,
54; *see also* COVID-19 pandemic;
post-COVID-19 pandemic
pandemic studies xvii, xviii, 2, 112–113
pandemic treatment: cleanliness and
42; conscious practices and 28, 34,
42–44; dilution by treatment trials
27, *27*; embedded sub-systemic
interrelations and 76–78; epistemic
methodology for 56–68; God's
Will and 22; IIE-model and 21, 96;

integrated medicine and 24–28;
inter-variable complementarities
43–47, 50; Islamic values and 13,
15; knowledge-induced parametric
model 94–95, *95*; lack of cooperation
in 112–113, 117n3; medical science
and 47; moral inclusiveness and
21, 28, 34, 42–43, 63, 68, 118;
multidisciplinarity and xviii, xx;
multivariate vector and monetary/
fiscal effects 57–59; neoclassical
economic approach 94–95, *95*;
prophetic guidance and 43, 52n14;
reconstruction of mutations and
20–21; restoration of normalcy 45;
science-economy-society moral
inclusiveness 63–64, *64*, 73, 77–78;
socio-scientific 47; Tawhidi law and
xvii, 2, 10; technological solutions
and 21; time variables in 106–107;
unity of knowledge and xx, 26–29,
42, **48**, 55; vaccines and 21, 112,
121; wellbeing and 3–4, 6, 9, 42–46,
51, 55, 83–84, 96–97, *97*
Parramore, L. 124
phenomenological consciousness 11,
31, *64*
political economy 74
post-COVID-19 pandemic: epistemic
consciousness and 2–3; Fourth
Industrial Revolution (4IR) and
118–119; moral exclusiveness and
17; moral inclusiveness and 28, 118;
restoration of normalcy 3, 10, 13;
socio-scientific reality and 2
poverty: disempowerment and 42,
52n12, 93, 107; economic growth
and 97–98; incapability and 100–101,
104–106; pandemics and 36, 97, 99–100,
100, 101, 104–107; rates of 93;
socio-scientific models and 85; trends
in 85–86; wellbeing and 41–42; zakat
(Islamic charity) and 35–36
Pratiwi, A. 9

Qur'an: on consciousness 31, 32n11;
doomsday scenario in 118, 129n2;
memorization of 12; on monotheistic
faith 53n18; on moral failure 10,
18n15; on natural medicine 28, 32n7;